TOO GOOD TO GO
TOO BAD TO STAY

Advance Praise

The last time I was married I was seeing 5 different therapists just to try and survive the marriage. After months and months of sessions and thousands of dollars I learned what is in this book that took me just a few hours to read. The author's methodology is accurate and her message is spot on. This book, like other "self-help" books require two things; one: read the book; and two, choose to put it into action. I was very nervous about putting my choice into action when I left my wife; everything seemed to be larger than life and so did the perceived negative consequence of my choice. The actual outcome was quite different and I have never been happier, healthier and at peace. Had this book been available 7 years ago I could have saved a lot of time and a lot of money by just buying the book.

—**Corky Byer**

This easy-to-read self-help guide to transforming oneself to make life-changing decisions is informative and comprehensive. Joanne King's knowledge and experience as a psychotherapist, healer, and coach shines throughout.

While this book will answer many of the questions any of us may have had or have about our relationships, the focus of 'Too Good to Go, Too Bad to Stay'" is to help those who are trapped in a toxic relationship, find a window of hope for changing their situation for the better. Through the straight-forward step-by-step practice of GRACE (Growth; Resilience; Authenticity; Conscious Choice; Embracing Change), Joanne King M.A. offers readers opportunities to transform their lives so that they can make an informed decision about how they wish to navigate their ongoing journey in life.

—**Yolisa Duley**, Ph.D

This is a must read for all women. While I am blessed not to be in a toxic relationship at this time, I felt in many ways the author was speaking to me personally and I benefited from this book immensely. If you are in a toxic relationship, this book helps to identify the behaviors and signs and provides profound insight in creating your own path to self-awareness.

—**Kim Bragdon**

This incredible book is a step-by-step guide that will transform your life. If you learn how to heal by practicing the exercises in the book, there is no doubt you will see yourself and the relationship you're in more clearly. Then you can decide if your relationship is too good to go or too bad to stay.

—**JW**

"We cannot begin to love ourselves without the understanding that the inner and outer are integral to each other." Ms King has written an easy to read and understand book that is packed with valuable information to help anyone not only assess their relationship status but masterfully guides them on how to move their life into GRACE.

—**Mardi Werner**

"Too Good to Go, Too Bad to Stay" is an incredible tool for anyone in a toxic relationship. It's easy to read and follow with clear steps to find your authentic self and ultimately decide whether to stay and work on the relationship or leave and create a new life.

—**Martha Maddi**

Joanne King's book, "Too Good to Go, Too Bad to Stay" is a self-help easy to read guide that supports and encourages not only in self awareness but self transformation when considering or changing ones' life situations. Joanne's extensive knowledge, experience and wisdom as a psychotherapist, healer, and coach demonstrates clearly her sensitivity and compassion in her patients' well being. The book is well organized with its straight-forward step by step practice of a GRACE (Growth; Resilience; Authenticity; Conscious Choice; Embracing Change), that opens the door with the hope of gaining back one's power thus the ability to change one's current situation.

—**Veronica Ianniello**

Too Good To Go Too Bad To Stay is a powerful journey through the confusing web of dysfunction into empowered liberation. Offering a dynamic set of tools and practices Joanne skillfully escorts the reader through the maze of confusion and conflict into a peace that will serve as a stable foundation for a whole and enriched new life.

—**Lesley Michaels**, author of *Just Roll Over and Float*

TOO
GOOD
TO GO
TOO BAD
TO STAY
5 Steps to Finding
Freedom From a
Toxic Relationship

JOANNE KING M.A.

NEW YORK

LONDON • NASHVILLE • MELBOURNE • VANCOUVER

TOO GOOD TO GO TOO BAD TO STAY
5 Steps to Finding Freedom From a Toxic Relationship

© 2018 **JOANNE KING M.A.**

Published in New York, New York, by Morgan James Publishing in partnership with Difference Press. Morgan James is a trademark of Morgan James, LLC. www.MorganJamesPublishing.com

The Morgan James Speakers Group can bring authors to your live event. For more information or to book an event visit The Morgan James Speakers Group at www.TheMorganJamesSpeakersGroup.com.

ISBN 978-1-68350-815-1 paperback
ISBN 978-1-68350-816-8 eBook
Library of Congress Control Number: 2017916180

Cover Design by:
Rachel Lopez
www.r2cdesign.com

Interior Design by:
Bonnie Bushman
The Whole Caboodle Graphic Design

In an effort to support local communities, raise awareness and funds, Morgan James Publishing donates a percentage of all book sales for the life of each book to Habitat for Humanity Peninsula and Greater Williamsburg.

Get involved today! Visit
www.MorganJamesBuilds.com

To all the women who have come before me,
and to all who will follow

TABLE OF CONTENTS

INTRODUCTION

*The most painful thing is losing yourself
in the process of loving someone too much,
and forgetting that you are special too.*
– **Ernest Hemingway**, *Men Without Women*

The most important thing in life is to love and be loved. Love is one of life's most basic and fundamental needs. We all desire to be loved, nurtured and cared for, by our significant other, and a good relationship makes us happy, fulfilled and empowered in our lives. On the contrary, an unhappy relationship can take the fun and joy out of life. It may include yelling, fighting, arguing and name-calling, and your intuition may be telling you that something is askew, but you just can't put your finger on it. You've likely picked up this book because your relationship may be feeling difficult and uncomfortable, and it may not be as fun as it used to be. When an argument ensues, you may feel there is a lack of communication and connection between the two of you. You may be getting blamed for everything that happens, and told to just get over your feelings. And while all this may be going on, you don't really know what to do. Can I make my relationship better? You wonder should I stay? Should I go? Is my relationship bad enough that I need to leave?

Toxic relationships can be difficult if not downright impossible to understand, and they are just as hard to identify since they leave no bruises or physical signs. Toxic relationship behaviors are insidious in nature, and slowly creep into our relationships. They may start with jealous rage or controlling behavior and can include, but are not limited to unrealistic expectations, isolation, blame, hypersensitivity, dual personality, criticism and contempt.

I want to help you get clear on whether or not you're in a toxic relationship, and if it makes sense for you to stay or go. This book is designed to help you free yourself from a relationship that just doesn't feel right. Within this book, you'll learn the skills and tools necessary to break out of a toxic relationship and into a relationship you've always dreamed of—the one that's a true soul's purpose with another. A relationship that embodies respect and dignity of two separate, yet interdependent people who create a deep loving partnership of the mind, body and soul. Using the GRACE methodology provided for you in this book, you will gain the knowledge and skills necessary to know if you can stay and make it work or if it's time to go.

When Lauren came to me, she was feeling lonely and unfulfilled in her relationship. "I spend so much of my time trying to be the perfect wife, and so much of my world revolves around my husband that I don't have any interests or friends anymore." As we kept talking, she told me that she was working very hard to keep her husband happy, because if she didn't, he would become angry and lash out at her. His angry outbursts would include name-calling, blaming, ridicule and character assassination. Lauren felt like she was constantly walking on eggshells. No matter how hard she tried, it was never good enough. It'd gotten to the point where Lauren was now abusing Vicodin as a coping mechanism to relieve her stress and the anxiety she was suffering from in her relationship. After working together and taking her through the GRACE method, Lauren was able to free herself from her toxic relationship.

This book will assist you in recognizing, understanding and gaining back your personal freedom and power. There are no shortcuts, but with the GRACE method, you will be able to step into greater self-awareness, and transform and create healthy, loving relationships, and a life that you love.

Embracing the GRACE methodology will help you:

- Focus on what's truly important to you
- Release stress and emotional pain
- Create space for clarity
- Make conscious choices to support your health and happiness in life
- Experience emotional well-being
- Embrace your purpose and journey

- Embrace uncertainty and the courage to find your path
- Cultivate gratitude and self-compassion
- Discover ways to create healthy, loving relationships
- Observe yourself without judgment
- Connect to the happiness within
- Bring more joy and happiness into your life

Chapter 1

AM I IN A TOXIC RELATIONSHIP?

The tongue like a sharp knife…
kills without drawing blood.
–Buddha

Nancy is a 44-year-old mother of two who doesn't understand why she feels so bad and so frustrated in her marriage. She feels like she loves her husband, but doesn't get the love she needs in return. They were college sweethearts, and it was love at first sight. Dean was a handsome, charismatic, intelligent medical student, with a goal of becoming a plastic surgeon. They married while Dean was in his residency. Nancy imagined they would be married for life, since they had so much in common, including their college, work and friends. After they married, Dean began picking on Nancy, and bullying her in their relationship. Dean could be kind and loving one moment, and the next he would have angry outbursts, threatening and intimidating her. He called her names and belittled her in front of their children and others. Dean had been a good provider, and Nancy had depended on him for all these years. She tried talking to him, but his response was "if you don't like it, get the f*** out." Nancy felt hurt, heartbroken, sad and alone, and she began to believe the insults and hurtful names Dean was calling her. Nancy came to me very confused about her relationship, and looking for some clarity and understanding of her situation. She believed she loved her husband with all her heart and she couldn't imagine leaving him, but she also couldn't imagine how to begin to get the love she needs.

Being in a toxic relationship is difficult to recognize since the toxic behavior is slow and subtle in nature, and because it leaves no physical scars or bruises. In the beginning, it is difficult to comprehend or define what is happening in the relationship, but most people feel like something is off. In fact, they know something feels very wrong, but they cannot quite identify it.

A toxic relationship is never about one isolated incident; it's about the cumulative effect of months and perhaps years of criticism, contempt, bickering, and being constantly beaten down. You may feel like your partner is a Dr. Jekyll and Mr. Hyde: one moment charming and charismatic, and the next angry and condescending. This is a very common pattern women have shared with me. Another grievance I hear frequently is how whatever you do, it's never good enough, everything is wrong and that annoys him. He refuses to ever be pleased. All your friends tell you how lucky you are to be with him, but none truly understand what is happening behind closed doors. Behind those doors you may suffer from constant criticism, intimidation, angry outbursts, name-calling, blaming, disparaging remarks, sarcasm, angry jabs, humiliation, emotional manipulation, and many other damaging behaviors.

If all of this sounds familiar, and you recognize some of the behaviors mentioned, you may be in a toxic relationship. These relationships can be especially harmful toward one's self-esteem, because when you're in them, you lose it without even realizing it. You feel blamed for everything, and even though you know you don't deserve to be treated this way, you think it's not that big of a deal. Guilt, shame and sadness will prevail and it becomes a cycle. Living with this cycle day after day, you feel ashamed and are afraid to share your experiences with others.

We stay in toxic relationships for many reasons, some that are practical, even if they are not rational. Below are some reasons people stay in toxic relationships.

- A partner might make threats so it doesn't feel safe to leave
- A fear of being alone
- Finances
- It's difficult to know and admit to being in an unhealthy relationship
- Don't believe it's possible to muster the strength and courage to move out

- Hoping that he will change, and believing it when he says he will
- Social standing
- Shame surrounding divorce
- For the good of the children

My client Sylvia stayed in a toxic relationship much longer than she wanted to because of her daughter. When she finally got the courage to leave, she took her daughter out to dinner and told her about divorcing her father. Sylvia told me her daughter was 11 years old at the time, and her response to hearing about the divorce was, "Mom, I have been praying since I was 7 years old that you would leave Dad." Sylvia asked her why she hadn't shared that with her and her daughter responded, "I thought you were happy," and Sylvia responded, "I thought you were happy, too." This was an eye-opening moment for Sylvia, after pretending all those years to be happy, to now know her daughter was doing the same.

How do you feel?

There are many components to a toxic relationship, and no two relationships are the same. Becoming familiar with and learning some of the signs and symptoms of a toxic relationship will better prepare you to understand and acknowledge that you may be experiencing one. Know that there's no shame in this, and that we all find ourselves in unhealthy situations at times. The main signs of a toxic relationship include feeling controlled, manipulated and put down. It's important to connect with your feelings, to really understand your relationship and if indeed it's toxic.

For instance, do you feel bad after an exchange with this person? Are your conversations all about making them feel good and not anything about you? If this is the case, you may be dealing with someone who displays Narcissistic tendencies. These types of relationships are usually one-sided, and the person is most always in need of extra emotional support, while not providing any emotional support in return when you need it.

Is your relationship no longer any fun? Do you feel like he is controlling your every move? He may be trying to keep you isolated from your friends and family, and may at times display irrational jealousy over others. You may perceive this as a loving behavior, but when it crosses the line into possessiveness, it can be unhealthy. Keeping you away from family love and support is never healthy. He may even start blaming them for the problems in your relationship. The more isolated you are, the more you will lose touch with yourself.

Did your self-esteem disappear or plummet? Do you feel like you argue over inconsequential things, finally agreeing with them to just stop arguing? Do they constantly criticize, mock and taunt you? You feel bad about the names and criticisms, which eventually you internalize. These internalized feelings turn into shame, guilt and humiliation, which destroy your self-worth and confidence. Feeling overwhelmed, you begin to ignore your own needs, making choices that are damaging to your own well-being.

How are your energy levels with this person? Do you feel drained and depleted? You may be feeling worn out since you cannot be your authentic self. Do you feel pressured into doing what they want for you? If you are feeling pressured into drinking, drugs or having sex when you don't want to, these are all signs of a toxic relationship.

Do you feel like you're crazy at times with this person? If you are beginning to question your sanity, you may be experiencing Gaslighting. Gaslighting causes confusion and a distorted view of reality. For example they will deny things they said, you may hear "You're crazy, I never said that." Gaslighting will make you feel crazy, and consequences can include depression, insomnia and paranoia.

Keeping your feelings at the forefront of your attention can be the best indicator for you to help recognize if you are in a toxic relationship. Have you noticed if your behavior has changed? Have you started drinking or smoking more? Are your friendships at work and at home suffering? Are you curt with other people, when you never were before? These can all be signs you may be suffering in a toxic relationship.

Many people experience these types of relationships, but no one really talks about them. It can be scary and disconcerting since you're not really sure what's going on. But know you are not alone, and I am here to guide you through the process of understanding this type of relationship, and if you should stay or go.

Awareness is the first step in freeing yourself from a toxic relationship. Knowing that you are not crazy, but have recognized your situation can be empowering. Gaining back your power will help you to regain control of your life. It's a shifting of the mindset, and once you realize the taunts and threats mean nothing until you give them meaning, you can break free and regain control of yourself and your life.

Signs and Symptoms

Being able to identify a toxic relationship is the first step in learning how to heal and begin the recovery process. Some general signs of a toxic relationship include:

- Feelings of worthlessness—low self-esteem and confidence
- Blaming someone else for one's own mistakes
- Minimizing the other's point of view
- Outbursts of anger and rage
- Lying to avoid responsibility
- Lack of acknowledgment of another's feelings
- Humiliation of another through verbal comments
- Disparaging and condescending remarks
- Control and manipulation of the other person
- Ignoring the other person's feelings
- Withholding love and money
- Giving the other the silent treatment
- Critical judgment used against the other
- Having to walk on eggshells at home
- You are often the brunt of jokes
- Being called "too sensitive"
- Feeling anxious frequently
- Monitoring your phone calls and emails

- Monitoring your time and where you go
- Making decisions that affect the family without consulting you
- Showing disrespect and contempt toward you
- Swearing at you and calling you names
- Treating you like a servant—ordering you around
- Getting angry when his needs are not met
- Behaving like a spoiled child
- Using guilt trips and or shaming to manipulate you
- Being emotionally distant
- Being emotionally unavailable
- Refusing sex until he gets his way
- Having a Jekyll and Hyde personality
- Behaving differently in public
- Refusing to discuss issues with you
- Being jealous of your friends and family
- Having to be the center of attention
- Reacting to situations by blowing them out of proportion
- Belittling you, and putting down your intelligence
- Accusing you of being crazy
- Denying their abusive behavior and invalidating you

Understanding a Toxic Relationship

Understanding a toxic relationship and the behavior in this type of a relationship can be difficult. Most toxic individuals believe they don't have any problems, and the problems they do experience stem from the other person in the relationship. It is difficult to pin down the cause of a toxic relationship since every situation is different. Each person comes to the relationship with a different background and life experience. No two people are alike, and each case is different and distinct. In many cases, there have been influential adult role models in the toxic individuals' childhood that they are modeling, and who also taught them values through words and actions.

Some toxic individuals' behaviors can be traced back to childhood abuse, which occurred when they misbehaved as a child. They could have been emotionally or physically abused or neglected. The toxic individual may have suffered severe emotional pain from the abuse of power over them, and they suffer from a sense of failure and inadequacy. This misuse of power over a child can have a direct impact on their adult relationships if they have not worked through their emotional pain and hurt. They may take their experience as a child and turn it around in their present relationship, now acting as the person in control.

Many partners also exhibit anger management problems, which can co-occur with other conditions. Toxic individuals may feel freer to lash out verbally at another. If anger is an issue, they may be suffering from depression, too. Suzanne, another client, shared with me an example of how her husband Martin had an explosive temper. Her family was on a five-lane highway and a car cut them off. Martin was having none of that, and he sped up and cut in front of that car and stopped dead in the middle of the highway. Suzanne was 9 months pregnant at the time and thought she was going to die right then and there with her unborn baby. She was so frightened that a car was going to hit them from behind. Within minutes of Martin getting back on the highway, a state trooper pulled him over. Suzanne said she was relieved by the trooper's presence, and it seemed to deescalate the situation.

Most toxic individuals' behavior is caused by the fact that they have a deep insecurity and poor self-esteem.

My hope is for you to learn the signs and symptoms involved in a toxic relationship, and to help you decide if you should stay or leave the relationship. If what you read resonates with you and your experience, you are reading the right book. Throughout this book, I will provide you with the necessary space to determine what your next move should be.

Rarely do toxic relationships start out toxic. They usually begin happy and fun-filled with love and affection. The toxic behavior starts out slowly and expands into the relationship, and before you know it, you're in a relationship that you can't get out of. One way to work through the experience of being in a toxic relationship, and come to a place of clarity, is to practice mindful meditation. Throughout the book—at the end of each chapter—there will be a spirit work section. These sections will guide you through a meditation and other activities that will help you through the specific challenges we'll be discussing.

Practicing meditation is one way you can improve your happiness. Studies show that people who meditate are more satisfied in their relationships and their lives. Meditation is as simple as just finding a comfortable spot where you can just sit and be with yourself. It requires no special seat nor any types of props. You can spend as much time there as you like, but research suggests the more frequent the practice, the better. Even if it's only for a minute or two a day, it will be beneficial.

Setting a timer can be helpful to keep track of how much time you are spending in meditation. A mountain meditation is the perfect start to begin a shift in your life and relationships.

This meditation, along with all the others in the book, is offered on the Thank You page at the end of this book as a free download from my website. Just click the link for access to the free download.

Spirit Work

Find a comfortable seated position, and begin by dropping in on the breath. Long, slow deep breath in, and long, slow deep breath out. Close the eyes by bringing the upper eyelid down to meet the lower eyelid. As you're seated, begin to completely relax your body, relax your eyes back into your head, releasing the ears, releasing the jaw, following the breath. Long, slow deep breath in, and long, slow deep breathe out. Imagine yourself now in a beautiful meadow, between two mountains in a deep, verdant valley. The sun is shining and warming your face as you sit, relaxed, and your body is soft. Pay attention to any tension your body may be holding, and release the tension on your next exhalation. As you breath in and out, you notice the warm sun on your face as you breathe. As you are seated, you begin to notice that you embody the strength and stability of the mountains. Coming back to your breath, you begin a long, slow deep breath in, and long, slow deep breath out. Resting in awareness from moment to moment, breath by breath. Similar to waves in the ocean, you follow your breath in and out. You have no agenda, no place to go and nowhere to be except here in this moment, in this breath, in this moment.... Should you notice your thoughts coming and going, and that you're not focused on your breath, gently bring your attention back to your breath, embracing the full awareness of the breath. Knowing that our minds have a propensity to wander, and jump from thought to thought, always bring your attention back to the breath, to this moment with no judgment or harsh criticism. Always finding compassion and love for yourself in the moment, loving tender kindness toward yourself. As we begin to come back, gently opening our eyes, we can take the strength and solidity from the mountains and bring it into our lives, applying it to the many challenges we face, along with love and compassion for the self.

Chapter 2

TRANSFORMATION THROUGH GRACE

In the end only three things matter: how much you loved, how gently you lived, and how gracefully you let go of things not meant for you.
– **Anonymous**

I f you have found yourself in an unhappy relationship dominated by emotional suffering and dysfunction, know that you have the power to change it. Regardless of your past experiences, you have the opportunity to have the relationship you've always dreamed of. You may choose to stay or to go, but whatever your decision is, you will need to change the dynamic in the relationship. Fear is what holds most people back, and it can be challenging to overcome, but not impossible. Once you are able to move through your fears, you will be free to have the relationship you've always dreamed of.

GRACE is a 5-step method you can use to transform your situation with confidence and ease. Change is never easy, but having guidelines can help you find the right path. You will then be inspired to embrace your purpose and journey, no matter how difficult it may seem.

G—GROWTH
R—RESILIENCE
A—AUTHENTICITY
C—CONSCIOUS CHOICE
E—EMPOWERMENT THROUGH CHANGE

G—Growth is all about understanding your personal identity, and how that affects your self-image. Connecting with your authentic self will give you a foundational understanding of the power of self-awareness, and how to use it to your advantage. Connecting with your authentic expression of self will allow you to live your deepest truths and desires when faced with challenging situations. Improving your self-awareness by understanding yourself is the first step in making positive changes in your relationship to create more peace, joy and fulfillment every day.

Growing and connecting with your true self will allow you to adapt and flourish. It takes time, effort and commitment, along with a willingness to grow and learn. This provides an opportunity for developing your health, happiness, career and relationships.

Self-awareness is the first step in learning where you currently are, and then deciding where you want to be. Journaling about what you want to do to achieve your goal and go where you want to be will help with tracking your progress. Tracking your progress will also help you to become aware of anything that is standing in the way of your goal.

Melanie was angry and resentful toward her husband, Justin. He could be so cruel with his remarks, and he would have angry outbursts if Melanie didn't do what he wanted. She knew deep down inside that his behavior wasn't normal, and she began enquiring among her friends about their relationships. Most validated what she thought, which was that in a healthy relationship, one doesn't yell or beat down the other person.

Justin was adamant that Melanie was the one with all the problems, and made that clear by constantly telling her, "You are the crazy one, look at your family." Melanie knew he would never be open to change. She tried many times to bring reconciliation and mutual understanding to the relationship, but Justin always rejected it. Melanie was now questioning her own sanity, and knew she needed to change to have any sense of happiness in her life.

Having the understanding that we cannot change the way things are, but we can change the way we look at them, will help you to navigate through your issues. Use the challenges in your life to motivate you and help you to succeed.

R—Resilience is a quality that can be learned and helps people recover from trauma, hardship and stressful events in life. Resilient people perceive and see things differently and have the strength to respond more adeptly when faced with an issue. Resilience is built on feeling in control of your situation, while being able to act in response to a challenge. In this book, you'll learn how to nurture and facilitate resilience through meditation.

Seeing all difficulties as an opportunity to learn and grow will foster resilience in your life. Knowing that you are in control, and can manage these difficulties, will provide invaluable lessons, while building your confidence and self-esteem.

Moving forward into the unknown can be daunting. Who knows what is out there for you, and how you will grow and benefit from what you learn. If you decide not to move forward in life, you may miss opportunities to experience great things. You are the only one who can make a difference in your life, and your ability to manage the situation effectively will make all the difference in your outcome.

A—Living an authentic life is linked to happiness by knowing what is important to you. An authentic life is about being true to yourself, and living the life you were meant to. Faced with the fear of rejection if we express our true nature, we live lives that are not authentic. This causes a repression of our feelings, talent, creativity, and self-awareness. Feelings of anxiety in your life may be a significant message from your true self that you are not living your authentic life.

Using the GRACE method, you will discover how to pay attention to your internal dialogue through self-awareness and self-knowledge. Self-awareness comes from within, not from outside yourself looking in. You will learn how to connect with the messages and intelligence of your body, as well as with the clues and opportunities the universe is sending you. Tuning into all of these messages will guide you in the direction of your true path and the fulfillment of living an authentic life.

When you can be authentic with yourself, you are coming from a place of honesty and are able to communicate your true wants, needs and desires to someone you love. Living from this place will strengthen your relationships by allowing you to connect on a deeper and more intimate level. Authenticity also provides an opportunity for more meaningful dialogue that will facilitate a better understanding between two people. When this communication becomes blocked, one's truth is never revealed.

My client Tasha practiced mindfulness, cultivating her self-awareness. This allowed her to live from a place of honesty within her true self. From this place, she was finally able to understand that much of her unhappiness was from not acknowledging how she was living someone else's life. Yes, she had the big 4-bedroom home, with the 3-car garage and all the trappings that go along with that, but she was miserable. When she made the connection, she was able to make the decision to move out.

When Tasha told her husband James she was going to move out, James convinced her he was going to change, and everything would be different. Tasha, who trusted and believed him, decided to give him another chance. Within two weeks, James had an angry outburst breaking down their bedroom door. That was the end for Tasha, and she packed up her things, and their son, and moved out. It was a very difficult and frightening time for her, but something inside her told her it would work out and she would be ok. Tasha began to feel better and not so crazy anymore being out on her own. She was no longer subjected to toxic behavior on a daily basis, and had more energy to focus on things that were important to her. Tasha realized that life could be fun, and began finding joy and happiness by living her authentic life.

C—Every situation in life requires a decision that is borne out of a crisis, chance or *choice*. Think about how your current life situation is the culmination of choices that you've made sometime in the past, whether it was 30 minutes or 30 years ago. Now think about how your life may be a direct result of choices you didn't make. Many people have a hard time making a choice, and it's due to the terrifying reality that we are afraid of making the wrong decision. But is there really a wrong choice? We can never know this until after the decision is made and we have lived through it. Only then can we evaluate if it was a wise choice.

A Conscious Life

The choices we make in life can be conscious or unconscious. *Conscious choice* is the art of living our life creatively where we make decisions based on our thoughts, desires and aspirations. Living with unconscious choice can feel like drifting through life on autopilot, and not knowing how we got there.

Thinking about your decisions and making conscious choices is about taking control back in your life. Creating a conscious life is relatively simple to achieve once you become aware of the process and apply it in your life.

Leaving Ron was a conscious choice for Tiffany after living in a toxic relationship for 20 years. She organized a plan incorporating where she would go, and made sure she would have enough cash to sustain her until she could find a job. Tiffany also took important documents and other valuables she needed as she embarked on her new life. Tiffany asked for help and support from her many friends and family who were witnesses to her suffering. Most of her friends and family were happy to help her and be there for whatever she needed. They were happy to see she was finally making the choice to take control of the situation, and protect herself and her daughter by leaving. Tiffany felt good about leaving her unhappy relationship, and knew she was being a good role model for her daughter by removing herself from this situation.

When you begin to consciously look at different areas of your life, you will begin making decisions that you feel are right for you. As you practice conscious choice, it will become easier, and you'll grow more confident of your choices.

E—In each moment of life there is only one thing for certain: change. Empowerment through embracing change is a key element to grow and learn in life, but can be scary for people. Without embracing change, life will be stifled and a constant struggle. Using the fundamentals we discussed about growth, resilience, authenticity and choice can make embracing change easier, which provides a foundation for empowerment and well-being.

Embracing change was paramount to saving my client Maggie's relationship. Finding her voice through empowerment helped her to make the critical choice of asking for change in her relationship. It was only after Maggie was able to take back her power that she got her husband to embrace change in their relationship.

Maggie did not want to leave her relationship, but knew it would not be easy to get Dennis to change. After completing the GRACE method, Maggie felt empowered and began to make demands for change. Maggie began by telling Dennis "You are important to me and I want you in my life, but I cannot tolerate toxic behavior any longer." Following that, she sat down with Dennis and stressed how important it was for her to stay in the marriage, but she couldn't if he didn't change. It was important for Dennis to understand how serious she was, and just as important for Maggie to know that she would be okay if she left. Maggie started by setting boundaries with Dennis about what behavior she would accept and what she wouldn't. This was mind-boggling for Dennis, because he was used to his toxic behavior being accepted all the time. Maggie felt empowered, and knew that she finally had some control in the relationship and with her own emotions, reactions and actions. Maggie was able to facilitate positive change in her relationship by letting Dennis know that she only had the best intentions for him, her and their relationship. Through clear communication of her wants and needs, Maggie was able to save their relationship. They are still married today, and are always working together to make their relationship the best it can be.

Practicing the 5-step process of GRACE will help you clarify whether to stay or leave your relationship. In life we are all awarded choices, and making them from your most authentic place will allow you to know what the best decision is for you.

Spirit Work

Begin by setting an intention for this meditation. It may be to find a deeper connection with your true self, open yourself to change, or to grow in wisdom when faced with challenging choices. Think about what the perfect relationship would look like, and envision it as you sit in silence through this meditation.

In a comfortable seated position, close your eyes and begin to breathe deeply. Begin to feel the in-breath and out-breath. On the inhalation, breathe in relaxation and, on the exhalation, release any tension you may be holding. Repeat the in and out breath for at least 5 cycles. Allow any thoughts or tensions of the day to fall away. Feel the muscles of your body relax as you let go of any physical tension. Especially the muscles of the jaw and eyes. Any areas that you notice you may be holding tension.

Focus on the breath as you breathe in and out. Letting it flow smoothly, breathing in from infinity out to infinity. Keeping your awareness on the breath as you become one with the flow of life, and at one with your being. As you breathe, in from infinity and out from infinity, and as you do so, become aware of the place within, the place where you are most yourself. The center of your being. This is the real you beyond the thoughts, drama and identifications of the mind. As you breathe, connecting with this place, your authentic true self. Feel the awareness of knowing you are connected with your true spirit. Now as you are breathing, begin to ask your authentic self what is the most important thing to you in your life? What does the perfect relationship look like to you? What are your values in that relationship? Take a few breaths to contemplate the answer to these questions.

Coming back to your authentic self, this is the person who you truly are, who you can truly be with no one to hold you back. Visualize yourself as this person you recognize and begin to strip away anything that is holding you back from being this authentic person. Begin to strip away fear, doubt, self-loathing, guilt, shame and anything else you perceive to be holding you back. Watch as all these issues that were at the forefront of your person dissolve… and go away.

Your true self is now left, freedom from all the encumbrances of negativity. Your true self now has the freedom to emerge, and bathe you in the white light of love and compassion, as you sit breathing in and breathing out.

Know how you can now move forward in your life free of all negativity and at peace with yourself. Breathing in and breathing out for 5 breaths or longer if you choose.

Spirit Work 2

Reflecting on what was important to you as you meditated, let's create a vision board. Here is where you need to tap into your creative Goddess. Your vision board will be a visual map for you to create your best possible future. Start by imagining the relationship you've always dreamed of. The perfect life, partner, home, automobile—anything you like is possible on your vision board.

Begin by choosing three to five magazines, perhaps new or old favorites. As you go through them, only look at the pictures and choose the pictures that most appeal to you. Lay them out in different layouts, then choose the layout that most resonates with you. As you begin looking at your layout, ask yourself a few simple questions:

- Do you notice any reoccurring themes?
- Compare the vision board pictures with your current life. Are they the same or different than your life now?
- What type of qualities does the vision board represent?
- Make notes of what the pictures represent to you and be specific.
- Think about why you would like your life to be like this.

Chapter 3
GROWTH

Our greatness lies not so much in being able to remake the world as being able to remake ourselves.
– Gandhi

Self-awareness and personal development is necessary for us to understand what is behind our attitudes, thinking, reactions and interactions with others. It is through the powerful impact of growing, knowing and understanding ourselves more deeply that we develop emotional intelligence, which helps us in all aspects of our life and relationships.

Self-Awareness

Understanding and gaining self-awareness is the first step in the healing and recovery journey from toxic relationships. Healthy relationships do exist and you deserve to be in one. You may be able to work through the issues in your current relationship, or you may choose not to. Whatever your decision, it's important to have the knowledge, tools and self-confidence to take back your power.

Self-awareness (also known as self-knowledge or introspection) is all about understanding your own needs, desires, and feelings and having a clear perception about your character. Relationships are vulnerable to many ups and downs, and when you have an absolute understanding of your own self-awareness, you are in control of your emotions. It is through control of your emotions that you can easily begin to understand others, and how they perceive you, and how you respond to them by controlling your emotions and reactions.

Practicing skills to develop self-awareness is critical in moving forward toward living your authentic life. When you are able to focus your attention and your emotions, you begin to take back your power. Self-love is another aspect of self-awareness, and a crucial element in guiding you to live the life you've always dreamed of. Once the veil is lifted and you see your true inner beauty and strength, you will move forward in life as the warrior Goddess you truly are.

By paying attention to your thoughts, emotions and behavior you can develop self-awareness. Mindful meditation—and specifically the practice of loving kindness—is one way to strengthen your self-awareness. Practicing loving kindness will help you to show more compassion and love toward yourself. This allows you to become the compassionate witness in your life, providing wisdom for you in times of turmoil. You are able to listen to the kind, wise, non-judgmental voice in your head who provides love and compassion instead of the angry critical voice in your head. When you are less judgmental of yourself, you begin to become less judgmental of others, which means you can begin to see your relationship differently. These qualities are the keys to understanding and learning if your relationship is right for you, and if you want to stay or go.

Metta or Lovingkindness

Lovingkindness or *metta* is a Buddhist term for benevolence, fellowship, goodwill, unconditional love and wisdom. Lovingkindness meditation is a meditation that provides feelings of love, while opening our hearts to connect with oneself or others in a positive loving way. There are no conditions or restrictions on lovingkindness, or expectations of anything in return. The main tenet of practice is pure love. By creating self-love and compassion for ourselves first, it allows us to have the capacity to share it with others. Without this unconditional love and acceptance for ourselves, we cannot share it with others.

Lovingkindness meditation provides us with a sense of acceptance and love. This diminishes the judgmental tendency of our mind, and allows us to be open and accepting of others and ourselves. The foundation of lovingkindness practice is pure love, the nature of our being. The practice is about opening the heart to kindness and deeper feelings of love, from a place of selflessness. It is a practice of breaking down barriers within us, and then toward others.

Practicing lovingkindness in life when faced with severe difficulties takes patience and courage. Most often in life we seek happiness, and turn away from pain and unhappiness. In mindfulness, we are asked to turn toward our pain, bringing a caring, open attention to the suffering, hurt parts of ourselves. It's a bit of a paradox, but turning toward our pain builds strength and resilience as we fulfill the needs of our lives.

Practicing lovingkindness meditation will help to cultivate wisdom and happiness, while allowing you to become the best version of your authentic self. The meditation begins with a feeling of care, concern, lovingkindness, compassion and warm-heartedness toward oneself and then others. The practice encompasses six categories that expand and develop lovingkindness from ourselves to all sentient beings. We express lovingkindness to all beings through the focus of our attention on each category. You may use the phrases here, or change them up to reflect your own personal lovingkindness experience.

Six Categories
We extend lovingkindness to all beings in this order:

- Ourselves
- A benefactor, or person who benefitted us
- A good friend
- A neutral person, about whom we have no feelings

- A person we find difficult or with whom we're in conflict
- All beings without exception

Traditional Phrases
You may use these traditional phrases or ones you choose:

- May I be free from inner and outer harm
- May I be safe from danger
- May I be happy
- May I be healthy
- May I live with ease
- May I be free of physical pain and suffering
- May I live in this world happily and joyfully

When beginning your lovingkindness meditation, you can use these phrases to extend lovingkindness to yourself. These phrases demonstrate our wish to experience safety, happiness, health, ease and freedom from pain and suffering. As you progress in your practice begin to wish these qualities for others by changing the "I" to "you." For example, "May you live with ease."

It's not uncommon to find it difficult to extend lovingkindness to ourselves. When our hearts have been closed for a long time, we may feel resistance to showing ourselves compassion and lovingkindness. As we practice, the resistance will begin to break down, but it can be a slow process and you may feel frustrated at times. You may also feel resistance toward showing lovingkindness to someone difficult in your life. In this case, you can include yourself in the phrase, "May we live with ease." Your heart will begin to open over time, and it will extend into all areas of your life.

Studies indicate that practicing lovingkindness has amazing benefits. This is one of the best ways to heal a troubled mind, freeing you of pain and suffering. If you would like to boost your happiness levels and develop skills to help with stress, lovingkindness will help you achieve that, along with the following 11 benefits that were first identified by the Buddha.

1. You sleep well
2. You awaken easily
3. You enjoy pleasant dreams
4. People love you
5. Celestial beings love you
6. Celestial beings protect you
7. You're safe from external danger
8. Your face is radiant
9. Your mind is serene
10. You will be unconfused at the moment of death
11. You'll take rebirth in the higher, happier realms

Mediation is one way to develop inner wisdom, and the more you practice, the more you will grow and flourish. Our focus has been on formal practice, but there is also an informal meditation practice.

In your daily life, you can bring informal practice into almost everything you do. It only requires open and accepting awareness to your full range of experience unfolding around you.

When your focus changes from doing (planning, analyzing) to be-ing (sensing, feeling) you can fully engage in the moment. It's simple and requires you to just feel your breath, your bodily sensations and your experience in the moment. Being present moment by moment, breath by breath.

The truth is we are beings greater than we can comprehend. As Marianne Williamson puts it, "*Our deepest fear is not that we are inadequate. Our deepest fear is that we are powerful beyond measure. It is our light, not our darkness, that most frightens us. We ask ourselves, 'Who am I to be brilliant, gorgeous, talented, and fabulous?' Actually, who are you not to be? You are a child of God. Your playing small does not serve the world.*"

Learning to love yourself will take you into the greatest relationship of your life. It will improve and change all other relationships. We cannot settle for less. Liberate yourself from the negative self-critic in your head, and begin to love yourself from a place of compassion and loving kindness. You may experience many dark moments filled with pain and confusion, and when this occurs, know that you are on the right path to finding your inner truth.

"*We must pass through the darkness, to reach the light.*"
– Albert Pike

Feeling your emotions is key to self-enlightenment. Our minds inner critic often torments us with feelings of guilt, shame, and self-loathing. These thoughts may look like "I'm not good enough," "I hate myself," "I'm not skinny or pretty enough," and on and on. It is just these types of thoughts and emotions that we need to learn to accept and acknowledge through our mindfulness practice as a compassionate witness. Acceptance and acknowledgment of the thought and feeling—while remaining detached—is the first step. Following detachment, we release the thought with the understanding that it does not reflect who you truly are. Recognizing that these thoughts and feelings are a manifestation of our conditioning helps us to realize that they are transitory in nature. We identify a lot with our thoughts, but they are just thoughts and not truths. When we are able to put space between our thoughts, we are able to let them come and go. Our minds can cause us so much pain, but once we understand our thoughts are not truths, we have the power to change them and open our hearts to ourselves.

Friends in our lives give us a feeling of being supported and loved by another. Qualities of good friends include trust, loyalty and being a confidant. Friends can cheer us up when we're feeling bad, and they are always there when we need them. Good friends epitomize love, kindness and understanding. They are never judgmental. Wouldn't life be amazing with a friend that embodied all of these qualities? You have one in yourself. You are the treasure you seek at the end of a rainbow. Begin to respect, honor, love and support yourself, like your own best friend. Be there for yourself without self-judgment. When you begin to judge a situation as good or bad, begin to look at it as neither good nor bad. It just is.

When we learn to love others, but do not love ourselves, it becomes codependency. Codependency can mean many things, but basically describes a relationship that forms around a dysfunction. A person in a relationship without self-love experiences a deeply ingrained insecurity, which manifests in the form of loneliness, shame and fear of abandonment. Boundaries between individuals become blurred, violated or nonexistent. Self-love is the cure to a codependent relationship.

We cannot begin to love ourselves without the understanding that the inner and outer are integral to each other. Finding and cultivating inner happiness will lead to outer happiness. Inner happiness is found through self-esteem and a sense of self-worth. It's a feeling of security and being loved, without someone having to say the words. Outer happiness is dependent on external events, others and material things. Ideally inner and outer happiness should exist in one's world, balanced.

Awareness through self-love can provide a foundation to soothe our souls, by creating love and compassion for the self. The benefits of being kind and loving to oneself can be astounding. You may sleep better, lose weight, or perhaps even begin to be more social. This journey will take you deeper into who you really are. Only then can we begin to see our true power and connection to spirit.

Developing your inner spirit through mindful meditation and mindful movement will profoundly change your life. It can bring serenity and happiness and provide a strong foundation, enhancing all aspects of your life. This acceptance and love of self can provide the motivation necessary to move forward to the next step—whether it's to begin an exercise program, take up healthy eating, or make the decision not to be in a toxic relationship.

Working toward self-love will take awareness and alignment with spirit and our authentic selves. It is only then that we are able to give and receive love without being resentful and exhausted toward others and ourselves. Awareness of self-love provides the understanding that we are truly deserving of receiving happiness, respect and love.

Love yourself every day in ways that are important to you. Reflect on what you would expect someone else who loves you to do, and then do those things for yourself. Begin to treat yourself to things you enjoy, perhaps flowers or a small gift. Maybe even a nice dinner out. You may even want to go dancing with your new love interest. The love you can give to yourself will allow others to love you as you do.

Positive self-talk can be inspirational and motivational. There are many mantras one can say, but the best will mantras will be ones you write yourself. Write a love letter to yourself, and list all your beautiful qualities. If you cannot think of any, then write qualities that you would like to have. Once you identify these qualities, you can write your mantras from them. Examples of mantras include:

- "I love myself—I am perfect the way I am"
- "I love my body, and am grateful for the movement it provides"
- "I can be happy and healthy at any size"
- "I can trust my inner choices"
- "I am strong and beautiful"

The Goddess You Are

Treat yourself like the Goddess you are. Choosing the right foods for a healthy diet can do wonders for the mind and body.

Getting the right foods from each food group can improve your mood and enhance your body. Try to avoid excess alcohol, sugar, fats and salt. Eating right, exercise and overall physical care will add to your mental and physical well-being. Using your intuition and knowledge base of healthy foods, choose foods you know will make you happy, while keeping you healthy and fit. Moderation is the key without deprivation.

Letting Go Of The Past

Suffering from past traumatic life events can keep us stuck and unhappy. It's time to let go of any emotional suffering and move into the here and now. You may need the assistance of a counselor to move past your pain, or you may be able to work on it yourself. The memories you have will always be with you, but if you know and understand that's the past, you can begin healing, since they no longer will have a hold on you.

Our brains have the capability to build new pathways through neuroplasticity. What that means is our brains can heal themselves. The brain can begin to heal by rewiring itself from the negative emotions associated with a memory. By releasing the emotional pain from the experience, and focusing on positive associations, one can begin to move on. Focusing on new and good experiences will provide a pathway to begin healing.

Gratitude is one of the best ways to express positivity and happiness in our lives. By showing gratitude and appreciation for things in your life, research shows you can become happier and healthier. You may want to begin by journaling all the things you are grateful for. When I wake up in the morning, I like to immediately think of three things I am grateful for, and take them with me throughout the day.

Show appreciation to others in your life, even if it is for something small. Write them a quick note or call them on the phone, or perhaps tell them how they make the world a better place. People value the time you spend writing or visiting them. As an added bonus, you will feel uplifted from time spent with them and the positive feelings exchanged.

Spirit Work

Begin in a comfortable seated position. Relax and feel at ease in your body and mind. Gently close your eyes, bringing your upper eyelid down to meet your lower eyelid. Dropping into the breath, begin to follow the in-breath, and out-breath. Long slow deep breath in…and long slow deep breath out. Picture yourself now out in a large field, sowing seeds of intention as you sit relaxed. Don't force anything; just be present in the moment.

Start by opening your heart to yourself. Directing a sense of loving care, friendship and kindness to yourself. Think of one thing you like about yourself. It could be a quality or virtue, a part of you that you honor. Or perhaps think of something you have done that was respectable. For example, a time when you extended yourself to help someone who didn't ask for your assistance. If you draw a blank, remember yourself as a young child, and send lovingkindness to her.

If nothing comes to mind for either of these exercises, then just rest your mind in the awareness that you would like to be happy and healthy. Similar to other beings, you just want to be healthy and happy.

As you sit following your breath, acknowledge the good within you, or of your wish to be happy and healthy. Spend a few moments, focusing on the good within you or the wish to be happy and healthy.

Think of three to four phrases that would identify and express your deepest wish for yourself, not just for this moment, but also in a deep and lasting way. What is it you would most wish for in your life?

Begin with repeating the first four phrases:

- May I be free from danger
- May I be happy
- May I be healthy
- May I live with ease

As you repeat each phrase, let it come directly from your energetic heart center. Simply connect to it, and be with it. Don't force yourself to make anything special happen, just allow the phrases to be released. There may be moments of silence and that is ok, just come back to the phrases, letting them slide off of your tongue. Practice slowly and deliberately, and with no expectation.

In meditation, if you find your mind wandering, gently bring yourself back to this moment. Don't judge or analyze yourself, just gently come back to this moment and to your phrases.

When you feel you have a strong sense of lovingkindness for yourself, the next progression in lovingkindness meditation is bringing our attention to someone who is generally known as the benefactor. This person is someone who has taken care of you, been genuinely good to you, or perhaps helped you in some way. If no benefactor comes to mind, think of someone who inspires you. A person who is kind, loving, compassionate and who epitomizes all of these qualities. If no one comes to mind, continue with yourself.

Bring forth a visual image of this person, or perhaps say her name to yourself, and offer her the following phrases:

- May you be free from danger
- May you be happy
- May you be healthy
- May you live with ease

Gently open your eyes. Recognize and feel any bodily sensations. As you go through your day, keep these phrases in your thoughts, and continue to feel the power of lovingkindness.

Thought provoking questions to ponder:

- As you sent lovingkindness to yourself, what were you thinking? Did you have any images or feelings that came up?
- If you were sitting in a group of people who were all sending you lovingkindness, what do you think you would experience?
- What was the easiest part of the practice for you? And the most difficult?

Chapter 4
RESILIENCE

It's not hard to make decisions
once you know what your values are.
– Roy E. Disney

esilience is a quality that can be learned and helps people recover from trauma, hardship and stressful events in life. Resilient people perceive and see things differently and have the strength to respond more adeptly when faced with an issue. Resilience is built on feeling in control of your situation, while being able to act in response to the challenge.

Seeing all difficulties as opportunities to learn and grow will foster resilience in your life. Knowing that you have control and can manage any difficulty will provide invaluable lessons. Through practicing mindfulness, you can connect with your values, create goals, and practice self-care to strengthen resilience. One's environment can also play a role in resilience, and we will take a look at environmental self-care as a way to enhance your resilience.

Mindfulness Practice

Resilience can be achieved through mindfulness practice. Mindful introspection helps us to recognize how old patterns of behavior aren't working to enhance one's health and well-being. People who practice mindfulness (seeing things through the present moment) are better able to respond to stressful situations with wisdom. They also feel less overwhelmed and are better able to cope with difficult feelings and situations. It's not usually fear and anger that cause us problems, but how we react to these troublesome feelings. Without mindfulness, we can get caught up in these difficult emotions and more anger and fear will build as a by-product of reactivity in the moment. With mindfulness, we can recognize the bigger picture, and respond to the situation with a sense of equanimity and clarity.

Research has shown that mindfulness cultivates resilience, and is an important source of personal well-being. It helps to stop thoughts from ruminating and becoming obsessive, playing over and over again in your head. There are several key features to enhancing resilience:

1. Work at having positive relationships with family and friends. If you live away from family and friends, joining a social club or volunteer group can be helpful.

2. When challenges come up in life, look at positive ways you can deal with the issue.

3. Become more optimistic about life. Begin to look at all the good things in your life and show gratitude toward them. When you begin to think about the negative aspects of your life, work on only solving them in a positive way.

4. When an issue arises, instead of just waiting for an outcome without making a decision, be decisive and choose a response that will work in your favor. If you need support, call a trusted friend or family member to help you.

5. Know and accept that change in life is inevitable.

When my client Linda decided to make a change, it took courage and strength for her to tell her husband Jack it was over. He had a history of angry outbursts, and she was frightened and convinced he would beat her when she told him. On a Saturday morning she asked him to sit down, and she told him she wanted a divorce. Jack was stunned and didn't know what to say. Linda was shut down for so many years, never sharing her feelings with Jack, that he was shocked. He couldn't understand how she felt, and why she wanted to leave him. Jack was in denial about his toxic behavior and adamant about standing his ground. Linda knew that if Jack wouldn't change, she could not remain in the marriage.

Prior to deciding to leave Jack, Linda suffered from low self-esteem and low self-confidence and always doubted her decisions. Today Linda is flourishing, and able to stand up for herself through the self-awareness and resilience she worked to build through mindfulness, mindful movement and counseling.

Through practicing mindfulness and introspection, Linda learned that she was important and she mattered. She practiced the exercises in this book, and was able to share her feelings, learning about herself in the process. The most important thing she learned was that her feelings mattered and that she was not alone. The support she received helped her to face her biggest fears of telling Jack it was over and leaving him.

Values as a Foundation

Living a value-driven life can provide us with motivation to persevere through difficult times to reach our goals and dreams. Our values are like guideposts directing our life. They can create a sense of meaning in our lives, and guide us by connecting us with our authentic selves. When living life from a place of values, we live our truth and are able to reduce our suffering and struggles.

Many clients ask me, "What are values?" Values are the place we live from, our truth in how we interact with the world and our true essence. They are the attitudes, beliefs, strengths and qualities we want to stand for in our lives. They define the type of person you are. Examples of values include compassion, kindness, humility, connection, fitness, courage, humor and the list goes on. Values can best be described as your behavior in life. When your actions match your truth and what you believe in, you are living a value-driven life.

Living and honoring your values can make for a happy life. But how do we find out what our values are? It begins by connecting with ourselves through our mindfulness and mindful movement work. Grab a note pad to help identify your values. Here are a few questions to get you thinking:

- What really matters to you deep down inside?
- What strengths and qualities in your life do you want to improve and work on?
- What's important for you to take a stand for in your life?

Below are some additional questions to reflect and work on to determine your values.

- Reflect on the times in your life when you were the happiest. What was work and home life then? Who were the people you were involved with? What were the circumstances?
- Reflect on the times in your life when you felt proudest of yourself, both in your home life and work. Who were the people you were involved with? What were the circumstances? What else contributed to your feelings of pride?
- Now reflect on the times when you felt most content and satisfied, both in your home life and work. Who were the people you were involved with? What were the circumstances? What else contributed to your feelings of satisfaction in life?

Identifying Values

Looking back at all the experiences you identified contributing to your happiness, pride and satisfaction, think about what made them valuable and significant to you. Using Appendix A at the back of the book, identify 10 values from the chart that are important to you. Many of these values are associated with each other. For example, if truthfulness, integrity and straightforwardness were important to you, honesty would be a top value for you.

Look through your list and make a note of your top values. Prioritizing and knowing your values will help you when it comes to making decisions in your life. As you go through your list, compare the values two at a time, and choose the one you feel most resonates with you. If it is difficult, look at your two choices and imagine a scenario in your life where you might have to choose one. Putting your list in a top 10 order will help you to identify and understand which values are most important to you. As you review your list, ask yourself if you feel good about the values, and if the top three resonate with whom you truly are.

We make our decisions and choices based on our values. Personal values help us to grow and develop, and lead us toward our future. Our values are like an internal compass, always focused on leading us to finding happiness and satisfaction in life. Living from our personal values allows us to take control of our lives, so someone else won't.

Clients often ask me, "What is the difference between a value and a goal?" Our goals provide the direction we would like to go in life. For example, you want to stay with your husband, but cannot tolerate the way he emotionally and verbally talks to you. Staying with your husband is a goal, while not tolerating his toxic behavior is a value. Your most important value in this example is around self-protection. We haven't lost the value of being loving toward our spouse; we just prioritized what is most important. Another illustration is losing 10 pounds of weight; losing the weight is a goal, while eating healthy is a value.

No relationship is perfect, but when you are clear on what your values are, it can help when you are faced with a challenging situation. When you understand and know that your choices are congruent with your truth, your relationship will become stronger and you will be happier.

Goals

Are you living your life focused on your spouse or another? Many people become disconnected from their goals by living a life focused on someone else. When your life is focused on another, it takes you away from your own core values. You may feel exhausted from meeting everyone else's needs but your own. Do you notice yourself saying yes to something that makes you uncomfortable, but you do it anyway? It's important to understand your goals and values, and begin focusing on your strengths and qualities. You will become more honest about your feelings and what you do. How would you feel if you never had to do something again you really didn't want to do? I encourage you to connect with your values, and know what it is you want in your relationship. This will help you to gain clarity on making your decision of whether to stay or go.

Getting started writing goals based on your values can seem like a daunting process without some prior planning. Many clients of mine begin the process of writing down their goals (the most important part of goal setting), but do not do anything with them. Their goals were frequently too wide-ranging, not specific enough or just impossible. Clients also had a hard time with following through with their goals.

Setting SMART goals is an approach to use once you have clarified your values. Value-based goals using the SMART approach can help you make your goals a reality. S.M.A.R.T is an acronym for Specific, Measurable, Achievable, Realistic and Time-Framed.

SMART goals:

Specific: Make your goal clear and straightforward. Specify what actions you will take by answering the questions who, what, when, and where. An example of an unspecific goal: "I will not take this abuse any longer." A Specific goal would be "I will not tolerate verbal abuse, and when it begins I will take a stand and tell him how I feel and stop it."

Measurable: Think about how you will be able to measure your goal. Make sure you write your goals down so you can measure your progress, and keep track of when you complete them.

Achievable: Don't set yourself up for failure by setting a goal that is unrealistic. Choose a goal that is challenging but achievable.

Relevant: The goal should be important to you based on your life values.

Timely: To increase the likelihood of achieving your goal, set the most accurate time frame for you to complete it.

When setting value-driven goals, they can be considered immediate, short-term, medium-term or long-term goals. An immediate goal is one that is something you could accomplish within the next 24-48 hours. It is usually small and simple. A short-term goal is one that could be done over the next week to month, and a medium-term goal is one that could be completed one to three months. Finally, a long-term goal is one that can be completed within months to years, depending on the goal.

Be sure to keep your goals in writing, and set aside time each month to make sure you are working toward your goals. Reassess your goals monthly to make sure you know what is working and what isn't. If you find you are having difficulty with your goals, start to tune into your feelings and emotions behind the issue. Understanding what is holding you back, and tapping into the emotion, can provide strength for you to move forward.

Share your goals with family and friends. Their support can help you to stay accountable and to be more likely to complete your goals. Committing to your goals publically will help you to stay motivated. It may be uncomfortable at first to speak and share your goals out loud, but it will make a big difference in sticking to your intention.

You may face all kinds of challenges as you work toward your goals. It typically is never external forces that block us from achieving our goals; instead, it's our internal thought process of how we think, react and feel that can thwart our progress. Many people experience fear of change and failure when moving toward their goals. It can be uncomfortable, but being mindful and working through the discomfort will take you to the other side. According to the poet Robert Frost, "The best way out is always through."

Anytime when you are in the process of working toward your goals and you're feeling stuck, it's helpful to re-evaluate your choices, and reconnect with your values. This can reenergize you and you can begin again to work toward completing your goals.

Self-Care: Your Body as a Temple

When we are in a toxic relationship, it can be an extremely harmful environment. We may be sharing our home with a toxic partner, and living in an unhappy situation. Self-care is a critical component in helping to reduce stress, to increase self-confidence and to begin to focus on yourself. A healthy lifestyle can do wonders to empower your confidence and strength.

Rose was a traditional housewife in a toxic relationship for over 25 years. Her role was taking care of her family and running the household. When she came in to see me, she was at the end of her tether. Rose told me, "I feel like I'm going to have a nervous breakdown." Rose couldn't imagine leaving her husband, but wanted her life and relationship to change. Working with Rose, we began to focus on a self-care regimen, which included proper nutrition, exercise, mindfulness, self-compassion and a space to call her own.

Self-care was a concept completely foreign to her, and it took some time to develop a plan Rose could work with.

Part of her self-care was to create a sacred space. Rose carved a small space out of an extra bedroom and made it her own. She filled the space with sentimental items, and objects of beauty that she loved. There were flowers, essential oils, pictures of her family and items she collected on her travels. It was her own sacred space where she could find solace from her busy days. This was her space where she would come and focus on her own health and well-being. Here she was able to weather the bonds of transition, and begin to grow and evolve as her own person. Over time, Rose was able to become more assertive and self-confident. This translated into a happier relationship as she made her needs known. Rose was able to stay in her marriage, and make it better than she ever thought was possible—through focusing on self-care.

In our fast paced lives where we are always focusing on everyone else first, it's easy for us to neglect ourselves. When this happens, we lose connection with our self and can become unbalanced. In order to become stronger and live life on your terms, it's important to make yourself the priority through self-care.

Self-care is not about being selfish—it's about personal responsibility for one's physical, emotional, spiritual and mental well-being, through prevention and being proactive. Self-care may seem counterintuitive for some, but it can be empowering, energizing all aspects of life. Self-care encompasses practicing daily rituals and practices that help you to feel happier and healthier. For most of us, if we don't take care of ourselves, no one else will.

There are many benefits of practicing self-care, and they include prevention of dis-ease and illness. You will also feel better when you are taking time for your personal care. People who practice self-care feel more connected and productive in life. Recent research indicates that practicing self-care can prevent or reduce the course of a cold or flu and aid in recovery from cancer treatments.

Self-care is important in a number of ways. It allows us to feel like we have control over our health and well-being as well as having "me time" to take care of ourselves. Self-care can be anything that helps you to feel more grounded, connected and happy in life. Self-care can be about the small things in life, and you don't have to leave your home to practice them.

When we are in a toxic relationship, it can permeate all aspects of our being. Our stress levels are always heightened and our self-identity is compromised. Being less nurturing toward ourselves can lead us to feeling depleted, and at a loss for our mental and physical health. Self-care can fill this gap and provide an antidote to the emotional pain and suffering we are experiencing. This is foundational in beginning to heal and feel better.

Self-care is based on listening to your body and responding to what it wants. Your body is always sending you messages based on what it needs. You may begin to notice these messages through cravings, discomfort or reactions. Being in touch with your body through your mindfulness and mindful movement practice gives you an advantage to tapping into these signals.

Many things are considered self-care, including diet, exercise, sleeping, bathing, meditating, and yoga, just to name a few. Here are some suggestions for self-care, but I recommend you make a list of your favorite things and try to fit one in at least every day.

Self-Care:

- **A hot bath with your favorite essential oil and candle burning**: A warm bath can improve circulation in the body, while moisturizing your skin, hair and eyes. Bathing also acts as a calming agent for the nervous system.
- **Body brushing**: Dry brushing is an ancient practice that uses a natural bristle brush designed for skin. Benefits include improving circulation for the lymphatic system through stimulation, while helping the body to detoxify. Exfoliation through dry brushing is accomplished by removing dead skin cells; some people also claims it helps to reduce their cellulite (anecdotal).
- **Self-massage:** Find a massage oil that you love the scent of, and indulge yourself with a self-massage. Massage is one of the best ways to increase blood circulation and help the body detoxify.
- **Sleep**: Create a routine centered on sleep, and allow yourself to go to bed early. You'll be more productive, and feel good throughout the day.
- **Napping**: Can help you to reduce fatigue and increase alertness throughout the day. You may also experience better memory and increased performance.

- **Taking a walk outside:** Research indicates that walking in nature actually soothes the mind, and improves one's mood and mental health.
- **Gardening**: Gardening can help to promote weight loss, reduce stress, lower blood pressure and decrease depression.

There are so many ways to promote self-care in your life. Pay attention to the messages your body sends you, and recognize when you need to spend some down-time with yourself. Choose an environment that is tailor-made for you to relax, enjoy and de-stress. Then, when you're ready, you can come back into the world a new person.

The environment you create around yourself plays a big part in your wellness. As human beings we have a need for safety, security and physical comfort, but what about our spiritual comfort? Providing nourishment for your spiritual comfort will nurture your soul, and help in all other areas of your life. Making your home a respite from the rest of the world can help you to feel safe, secure and comfortable.

When you are feeling whole and fulfilled in life, you have the strength to make decisions from a place of clarity.

Clutter and the Spirit

Out of clutter, find simplicity. From discord, find harmony. In the middle of difficulty lies opportunity.
–Albert Einstein

In creating a space that nourishes your spirit, it's good to start by decluttering.

Clutter can add stress and chaos to one's life. At one time, you may have been in love with much of the stuff, but now it just overwhelms your home as well as your mind. When your life is stressful, and your home is full of clutter, decluttering can provide you with a sense of control and reduce stress. Losing the clutter will help you to make better decisions by simplifying your life. Improving your space by decluttering will translate into all areas of your life. You will become more confident in your decisions, and be able to see your way through even the toughest situation.

You may want to start with a plan if you have a large area or a whole house to work on. In that case, a dumpster may be helpful. Planning the process room by room will help you to feel accomplished as you move through the house. If no plan is in place, you may get frustrated and want to quit. I like to start decluttering by making three piles. The first one is the stuff I want to get rid of, and is usually trash. The second pile is stuff that I can donate or take to the thrift store to be recycled, and the third pile is stuff I want to keep. You may even be able to make some extra money by holding a garage sale with items of value that you have no use for.

By removing physical clutter, you are able to free up mental space and energy, returning focus, creativity and peace of mind to your life. Everyday we bring new clutter into our lives through the mail, shopping, magazines or items from work. Keeping up with clutter on a daily basis will help to keep your home well-organized and clutter-free.

Think about ways you can make a sacred space for yourself. Perhaps a space just for you, where you can just be. Such a place does not need to be big; it can be a small corner or a bay in a room. This is a space where you can come to escape from everyday life, and reconnect with your authentic self. Your sacred space is a place for you to gain perspective on your life by making it more meaningful.

This is your sacred space, and you can begin to make it all yours, by designing and adding items that having a special meaning to you. It will become your oasis away from the rest of the world. When adding items, think about your senses including smell, sight, touch, and sound.

Choose scents that you love, and that resonate with your spirit. Scented candles can add to the ambiance of a room in a subtle way, adding depth and character. Flowers also can be a beautiful addition for scents and some of my favorites are plumeria and tuberose. Essential oils—including lemon, lavender or rosemary—set in a diffuser can add a natural scent to a room.

Adding color to your space using flowers and greenery can be uplifting and energizing. Adding plants will also purify the air adding a safer, cleaner atmosphere. Lots of sunshine is always inspiring. You may want to add pictures of your loved ones, or places where you traveled and loved. Mirrors can transform a room by giving the feeling of added space and sparkle.

Adding silk, faux fur or other wonderful fabrics can enhance touch in your sacred space. Adding visual interest to the floor using rugs can be another way to enhance your space.

A fountain in the corner of your sacred space will bring soothing sounds of flowing water, and create negative ions that provide a sense of calm and relaxation. Chimes are also a great addition with their reviving, rejuvenating sound that brings you fully into the present moment. Create a playlist that will support your time spent in your sacred space. Perhaps music focused on relaxation and stress reduction. Choose music that is melodic and soothing for your soul.

Spirit Work

SMART Goals

Based on the values you identified in the earlier exercise, begin to write and develop SMART goals for yourself Take your time and think on what your hearts desire really is in your life and then write it down. You will be surprised how you can make your goals a reality by just writing them down, and focusing on them

Self-care

Continuing our spirit work begin to create your sacred space. Having a space that is an oasis to call your own will provide you with a space to relax and reconnect with your true self. Introspection is the key to a happier you. Follow the guidelines outlined in this chapter, and choose the items that resonate with you. Take your time and do a little every day. You will end up with the space of your dreams, and reduce the stress in your life.

Chapter 5
AUTHENTICITY

Authenticity is the daily practice of letting
go of who we think we are supposed to be
and embracing who we actually are.
— **Brene Brown**

L iving an authentic life can bring you more happiness because you're being true to your own spirit, character and self. By living from a place of true values and feeling comfortable in your own skin, you gain a confidence that is only obtained from within. Living an authentic life will provide for healthier and more sustainable relationships, because you are being honest with yourself and your partner. This will ultimately strengthen your relationship and allow a deeper connection on a more intimate level.

The challenge to living an authentic life comes in the form of fear. We fear being who we honestly are by sharing our real feelings about what is happening within us. In relationships we're afraid we may scare away others, hurt their feelings or perhaps they may even leave us. Forcing these inaccurate beliefs through our relationships results in living an inauthentic life.

Many times when we live life inauthentically, we somaticize our problems. We may experience symptoms of fatigue, body aches, headaches, stomach aches and so on. Risks of living an inauthentic life include anesthetizing with substances, externalizing problems through anger and internalizing issues causing depression.

By living authentically, we allow ourselves to be flawed and vulnerable. Setting boundaries becomes easier when we are living from a place of how we truly feel and what we honestly need. Living from a place of authenticity becomes easier the more we practice.

Alicia is a student who was in one of my mindfulness meditation groups. During our mindfulness discussion on authenticity Alicia shared the following. "I was angry with my husband about something, but I was afraid to tell him. I was afraid he would become angry and detached. So every day, I just kept this secret hidden from him, but it was growing, and I was becoming resentful and feeling disconnected toward him. He sensed the disconnection and asked me what's wrong, but I still wouldn't tell him. Finally one day, we got into a huge fight, and all the anger and resentment that built up exploded as I yelled at him. I know all of this could have been prevented if I had just been brave enough to tell him how I really felt."

Mindfulness is a practice that has profound importance in our lives. When we meditate, we can open up to what we are really feeling and what matters most to us. Staying present in the moment, getting grounded and connecting with your essential self is the foundation of an enlightened and authentic life. When we are caught up thinking of the past, it is simply a collection of memories, and causes us to feel depressed and empty. By contrast, when we think about the future, it only exists in our minds and may cause feelings of anxiety, fear and worry. By thinking of the past and future, we are ignoring the present moment and resisting what is, thus causing suffering in our lives. There is only the here and now to be fully and completely present with. This experience is known as mindfulness. Committing to the present moment and extricating yourself from the hold of the past and the pull of the future, brings oneself into living today without yesterday or tomorrow. Cultivating mindfulness provided Alicia with the insight she needed to understand she wasn't being authentic in her relationship. She understood that without the introspection she gained practicing mindfulness, she would have held onto the anger and frustration, and caused more pain and suffering in her relationship.

A mindful state has two basic parts. The first is self-regulation of attention, where one remains focused on present moment experiences. The second element is a mindset, which incorporates openness, acceptance, and curiosity to whatever arises in the present moment, despite whether the experience is pleasant, unpleasant or neutral. When we are rushed or busy, we lose sight of the present moment.

Mindfulness enhances and facilitates authenticity, and by cultivating self-awareness through mindfulness, we can begin to achieve the qualities of freedom to live an authentic life. Self-awareness knows what is genuine, how that feels and what it looks like. Understanding what your values are in life will help you to connect with your true self and what is important to you. Clarity on what matters to you in your life now will enhance your ability in finding authenticity. Living from this perspective can be empowering as your decisions become easier, and you make choices that are closely aligned with your values. It also becomes easier to embrace your imperfections, and know that these perceived differences are what makes you a unique and beautiful individual. People who live life through the lens of authenticity and their true self are more likely to live from a place of their values, and to work toward and achieve their goals. Connecting with our deeper authentic nature allows us to listen to our true self and create a life with meaning.

Mindful meditation gives us the ability to hear and connect with our authentic self. When we are able to sit in silence and listen, we can hear what is really important to us and live our lives from our own truth. Courage and strength are necessary when coming from a place of vulnerability in order to live your life wholeheartedly. Speaking what is in our hearts provides us with the opportunity to live our truth, and not be silenced by others. This is empowerment.

Through this mindset we are able to discern what our deepest desire is in regards to our relationship. Having the ability to connect with our authentic self provides what we need to know if we should stay or go.

Your New Best Friend

Emotional regulation is a quality that can be developed and will be an asset in your relationships and daily life. Have you ever had a moment where you said something to someone you immediately regretted? Or perhaps replied to an email in a flash, hitting "send," and then felt like crawling into a deep cyberspace hole? If so, emotional regulation could be your new best friend to take you from living mindlessly to mindfully.

These are examples of when our emotions control our mind, instead of our mind controlling our emotions. Emotional regulation is the ability to control impulsive and inappropriate behavior that is related to strong emotions. Key skills in emotional regulation involve:

1. Behaving in a way that is not emotion induced
2. Refocusing attention in the presence of any strong emotion
3. Being able to mitigate strong emotions that have been brought up
4. Automatic control of our emotions as well as conscious control

Mindfulness can help to train the mind to respond to emotional situations through awareness, with greater reflection and judgment in the moment. The goal is to experience emotions and reduce emotional suffering, which can ultimately occur through awareness and practice. Awareness begins with identifying your emotions. Simply naming and describing the emotions you are feeling can begin to help regulate them. Now that you have identified and understood your emotions, you can learn to cut down on the frequency of the ones you don't want. Start with reducing your unwanted emotions. Making positive changes in your environment and life will help to reduce the frequency of negative emotions. Recognize when painful emotions start and begin to change them. A fire is easy to put out when it is small, and the same is true regarding painful emotions.

Look at emotions not as good or bad, they just are. Repressing your emotions is not a good habit, and can be more damaging in the long run. Try and experience all emotions, whether good or bad, comfortable or uncomfortable, painful or pleasurable. Emotions can be helpful in your life when they are in your best self-interest, and when the emotion will bring you closer to your goal. They can also be beneficial when they influence others in ways that helps you. At times, our emotions will also send us messages we need to listen to. Paying attention to our thoughts, feelings and emotions will put you more in touch with your life. This will lead to making better decisions, and living a more enjoyable life.

Waves of the Breath

One of the most powerful ways to connect to the present moment is through the breath.

The fundamental nature of the breath as in life is that change is constant. Similar to the waves in the ocean, each breath is the same, but they are all different. Since the breath is invisible, we can easily forget it's there, but remember it's a vital component to sustaining our life. Focusing on the breath can bring us into a state of peace and power. Even for the shortest period of time, it can bring a feeling of calmness and serenity. For beginners, it is easiest to start by just noticing your breath, and breathing for two to three minutes several times per day whenever you have a moment. Sitting comfortably, try closing your eyes and breathing for a minute. Notice the sensations of your mind and the body when you are done. It can be particularly helpful to practice awareness of the breath when experiencing stress or anxiety, and will calm you down in the moment.

Using the breath as an anchor in mindfulness will help to cultivate your awareness of the present moment. You may begin to watch the breath coming in, and going out, by focusing on where you notice the sensation of the breath most. Are you observing the coolness of the breath as it passes through your nostrils, or perhaps you are noticing the rise and fall of the abdomen or chest. Wherever the breath is most prominent, focus on that area as you breathe in and breathe out. This will help to guide you back when the mind wanders, and allow you to be fully awake to what is already happening in the present moment. It doesn't have to be for a long period of time—in fact, just minutes a day will do.

Staying with the breath can be a difficult task, since so many things vie for our attention in our daily lives. When sitting and breathing, we can see just how busy our minds are. The analogy of a monkey mind is appropriate since our thoughts are usually jumping from here to there, and this monkey mind makes it difficult to stay present-focused. The monkey mind can be tamed through present-centered awareness and connecting with the soul through the body and breath. Begin with awareness of the monkey mind, and work at calming it down to reduce stress and anxiety.

When practicing mindfulness, we are working on our mind, body, and breath connection. As we sit connecting with our body, we become aware of it, and naturally begin to notice bodily sensations nonjudgmentally. As we bring these sensations into our awareness and attention, we do so without an agenda to changing anything.

Our bodies and mind are inextricably linked together, and one cannot go anywhere without the other. Bringing awareness and attention to our bodies provides us with a path to self-knowledge through introspection. Learning to pay close attention to your body can help you to identify feelings and emotions. Signals from the body that something is not right in your relationship might include constant headaches, stomach aches and a feeling of general malaise. Notice when you feel this way. Is it only with your partner? If that is the case, it could be a potential message from your body that something is wrong in the relationship.

Have you ever felt like you had butterflies in your stomach? Or perhaps, like you are carrying the weight of the world on your shoulders? These metaphors show you how your body can feel your emotions. It is through introspection that we can cultivate this connection with our authentic self, and begin to live the life we were meant to. When feeling lost or confused in life, this type of introspection can be helpful. Our mind and body are two very different related realities, and stopping to become aware of what you are feeling inside the body can help you to connect with what you are feeling in the mind.

As we connect with our body and mind, sometimes we may feel or sense the advent of something unpleasant, and the feelings of tension or pain associated with it. We may have been distracting ourselves from experiencing painful feelings and emotions by focusing on outside issues. Think about all the times in life when you wanted to escape painful feelings or bury them. Mindfulness reminds us to turn toward our painful emotions, while bringing a caring, open attention to them. These painful feelings become our greatest teacher in life, helping us to make wise choices. Being able to connect with your own authentic feelings will let you know if your relationship is helping or hurting you, and if it's time to go or stay.

Mindfulness for Difficult Emotions

Here are six steps to begin to incorporate mindfulness when encountering a difficult emotion:

1. Pause and turn toward the painful emotion
    i. Begin to take a few long, slow, deep breaths, pausing, and looking at the emotion you are feeling.
2. Identify the emotion you are feeling
    i. Are you feeling anger, sadness, or frustration? Don't try to repress or bury the feeling. Examine it with a feeling of openness and curiosity.

3. Acknowledge and accept the emotion and feeling
   i. Accept the negative emotion and what you are feeling by mentally acknowledging what you are feeling.
4. Understand the impermanence of emotions
   i. Know emotions are impermanent and they come and go. Look compassionately at what you are feeling in the moment and how you can take care of yourself.
5. Examine the emotion
   i. Think about what brought about the emotion and why you are feeling this way. Are your thoughts causing you to feel these painful emotions? Perhaps a family difficulty is causing you to think intensely about a situation causing you stress and anxiety.
6. Respond from your wise self
   i. Know you will always choose the wise response when you are able to think your response through, and understand the situation.

In mindfulness, we gently approach our busy minds without aggression or brutal action. Learn to observe your thoughts by acknowledging and accepting them and then releasing them. Trying to repress your thoughts will only make them come back all the more powerfully.

Without seeking your thoughts or trying to block them, just sit and watch them go by. Using a metaphor of a blue sky and white puffy clouds, I like to imagine a beautiful blue sky that represents the essence of your true self. As the white puffy clouds slowly drift by, I imagine putting each thought on a cloud as it comes up, and releasing it, letting it float away. There is no judgment and no agenda, knowing that our thoughts are neither good nor bad and they are not permanent. Know that thoughts are just thoughts, and you have the choice of whether to keep them in your attention or let them float away on the clouds. Continue, always coming back to your breath, breathing in and breathing out.

It can be freeing to understand that we are not our thoughts or emotions. Our thoughts are separate from ourselves, and are only mental events not to get caught up in. Having the ability to put space between your thought and your reaction will help to change your connection to the thought. It becomes easier to watch the thoughts come, and let them go. Others cannot make us feel anything or do anything. We are free to choose how we interpret and experience everything.

Let go of your mind and then be mindful.
Close your ears and listen.
– Rumi

Only with regular mindfulness practice and experience can we learn to separate ourselves from our thoughts and what is happening in our minds. When we are seated in mindfulness, we make a choice to sit, and be present in the here and now. Our minds may be telling us "you need to get up," or "think about this," at which time you may become irritated. But as we sit, we make a conscious choice not to accept and listen to these thoughts. As you put space between you and your thoughts, you will notice they will begin to lessen, and you will not be captive to them any longer.

Cognitive behavior therapy created the term "defusion" for the process of separating from our thoughts. It is the process of learning to step back or detach from your thoughts, images and memories. Instead of getting absorbed or dominated by our thoughts, we can let them come and go, just as we released them on the clouds. Stepping back and watching our thoughts pass by, we can understand they are nothing more or less than just words or pictures.

Mindful meditation has the capability to free us of habitual actions that cause us pain and suffering. Through the act of introspection through mindfulness, we are able to foster wisdom and love.

Begin to experience every moment with awareness and presence. This means being awake to experience every sensation or emotion in the moment, whether pleasant, unpleasant or neutral. Become the witness in your life, observing yourself experiencing these sensations, and living in the awareness of the ordinary. For example, if you are in line at the grocery store, be present with that instead of worrying about getting home and putting the groceries away. Leave the mode of action behind and come into the mode of being in the present moment. Experience the sights, smells and sounds of the grocery store. Feel the sense of peace and calm by being present in the moment.

Spirit Work

Begin in a comfortable seated position, noting your posture, keeping your back upright and straight. Embody a sense of dignity, with your shoulders moving down and back, and your chin is dropped ever so slightly toward your chest. Closing your eyes, drop into the experience of being here now and feel self-compassion and kindness toward yourself.

Focusing on the body now, in the present moment. Begin to feel your feet touching the floor, and the mat beneath you. Feel the sensation of contact with the earth and ground. Feel your hands on your thighs, resting comfortably, letting go of all stress, but staying alert and aware. Taking a few breaths here and releasing any tension you may be holding in, long slow deep calming breath in…long slow deep relaxing breath out.

As you breathe, follow your breath in and out, and once again finding your body, feel yourself here in this moment, breath-by-breath and moment-by-moment. Focus on the space right above the heart, the place where the energetic heart rests. When you breathe, breathe through that space, letting the breath circulate through the entire body. As you breathe, you become more relaxed and more at ease. As you relax, it becomes easier and easier to open up your imagination. Begin to imagine another you standing in front of you. This is the most magnificent you; this is your authentic self. Take a moment to feel totally at ease with your authentic self. Feel happy as this is who you truly are. Look at the way the authentic you stands, breaths, smiles, how they talk, how they walk, how they interact with others. Feel how the authenticity can assist you in handling any issues and any of your goals in life. Take a deep breath through your energetic heart and hold it in for a moment and now breathe out. Now step into and merge with your authentic self, where the two of you become one. See through the eyes of your authentic self, hear through the ears of your authentic self, and feel how good it feels to live life as your authentic self. Visualize and imagine how your life is different now when you live from your authentic self.

Now coming back to your breath and breathing normally, allow your breath to be…just be natural as you breathe in and breathe out. Notice each breath in and each breath out. Are you sensing the breath from within as you breathe in and breathe out? As you breathe in and out, imagine with the in-breath the calming quality attached to the in-breath, helping you to feel calm and loved, and on the out-breath feeling the relaxing quality of the out-breath with a sense of compassion and care attached to it.

Coming back to the present moment, open your eyes. Feel the sensations of the body and notice what you are feeling. Take this feeling of living with your authentic self through the rest of your day.

Chapter 6
CONSCIOUS CHOICE

Should I Stay or Should I GO

*A life lived of choice is a life of conscious action. A life
lived of chance is a life of unconscious creation.*
– Neale Donald Walsch

C onscious choice is about self-awareness, and its critical
importance in making the decision to stay or go in
a relationship. Self-awareness are the behaviors and
feelings that influence us in our day-to-day lives. The more self-
aware we are, the better we are able to understand ourselves. This
understanding improves the choices and decisions we make in

our lives, which ultimately leads to improved relationships and a more fulfilling life.

Using strategies to improve your self-awareness will help you with conscious choice.

This is where the real work begins: with listening and trusting your inner self. Learning to recover from a toxic relationship begins with trusting your own feelings and perceptions of reality. If your partner has been invalidating your feelings and perceptions, know that you are not wrong, but something is wrong with the relationship, and it's not you. Only when you connect with your authentic self will you know if it is right for you to stay or go in your relationship.

As you work toward conscious choice, you may begin to wonder how you ended up in a toxic relationship. Working toward freedom from being in a toxic relationship may trigger feelings of sadness, grief and trying to understand the dynamics of why it happened. This is a complex question to answer, but begins with our earliest experiences. Early childhood is formative in our development, and lays the groundwork for how we will cope with issues and relationships later in life. Early childhood relationships not only affect our perceptions of how we are being treated, but how we treat others.

When repressed emotions and memories associated with childhood traumatic events are not healed, they will pop up at a later time when least expected. As children, we did not possess the proper coping skills to handle the traumatic event, thus we formed maladaptive coping skills that we still use as adults. Many of our current experiences may be projections of our childhood onto others. For example, if your partner wanted to go out without you, you may be feeling rejected, similar to when you might have been rejected as a child.

We feel comfortable with what is familiar and predictable in life, and we find change uncomfortable. If there is a pattern in your life that keeps repeating over and over again, you may be functioning from a past trauma. On a subconscious level, we believe somehow we can finally make the past right. If we say the right thing, dress better, act nicer or make some other behavioral change, our partner will no longer taunt or criticize us. They act as a stand-in for the toxic parent or caretaker from the past. This past conditioning has led us to seek out abuse in our lives either consciously or unconsciously.

Being able to take control of your life—and recognizing the times that you are functioning from the past—is the first step in learning how to separate your subconscious negative biases from your current reality. Awareness of your history and patterns of thinking will reveal how they have a negative impact on current relationships. Symptoms that show up as an adult that indicate you may be suffering from childhood trauma include the following:

- Feeling numb or being cut off from your feelings
- Feelings of emptiness
- Being easily overwhelmed or discouraged
- Perfectionism
- Over-sensitivity to rejection
- Lacking clarity on expectations for yourself and others

Coping Strategies

Coping strategies we adapted as children were the way we learned how to survive. As we transitioned into being an adult, these childhood coping skills hindered our development of more appropriate coping methods. Childhood coping skills can also work against a person in developing their sense of self-concept. This leads to a deficit in learning how to handle and approach life's difficulties. Avoidant childhood coping skills are unhealthy when used into adulthood. They include two main categories:

1. Fight or flight, which includes hyperarousal, vigilance, defiance, resistance (freeze), and aggression
2. Avoidance behaviors including compliance (appeasement), disassociation, and fainting

Finding effective coping strategies will help you work toward repairing and managing past childhood trauma, and will benefit all your current relationships. You may find that some strategies work better than others for you in reducing stress and managing life issues, depending on the situation. It may be helpful for you to begin to write down your stressful situations and then a coping strategy you think may work. Keep a record when stressful situations occur and how well your strategy worked for future reference.

Here is a list of positive coping strategies:

• Take time for yourself: set aside time every day for yourself to relax

- Practice meditation and relaxation techniques: deep breathing techniques and progressive muscle relaxation are great stress relievers and promote relaxation
- Physical activity: getting your heart rate up helps the body to release endorphins (the body's feel good hormones), and provides the body with stress relief
- Friendship: having friends who are willing to listen and be supportive is critical in good times and bad
- Humor: adding laughter can lighten up any stressful situation
- Hobbies: having a creative outlet helps to relieve stress
- Nutrition: providing your body with essential nutrients improves physical and mental health
- Sleeping: the body needs time to rest and recuperate after a stressful day
- Pets: pets can help to reduce stress by taking your mind off of stressful events and situations
- Spirituality: recent studies indicate having a divine presence in one's life can have many mental health benefits.

Negative coping skills can impede your progress in dealing with stress. They include the following:

- Drugs
- Excessive alcohol
- Self-mutilation
- Repressing hurt feelings

- Excessive working
- Avoiding problems
- Sedatives and stimulants
- Denial

Negative coping strategies are not long-term solutions and provide only temporary relief. They will not solve your problems, and may only make them worse.

Working on coping strategies includes building self-esteem and self-confidence. Here are some suggestions for helping you to find the right coping strategies:

- Start by making a list identifying your strengths and weaknesses, and build on them to be the best you can.
- Family and friends can be a huge source of comfort and support, so make sure you make time for these relationships.
- Learn to accept kindness from others, and to remember the positivity offered by others.
- Just as your friends are there for you in your time of need, be there for others when they need you.
- Finances can place an undo amount of stress on our lives, so implementing and maintaining a budget can help to alleviate a lot of stress.
- Find a local organization where you can volunteer your time and talents. When we can get out and help others, it has a tremendous impact on our well-being.

- Seek out others who have had the same problems as you, since they can be a source of inspiration and solutions.
- Tune into your moods and feelings, and perhaps keep a journal to learn how to deal with your emotions and express yourself.
- Learn to be at peace with yourself, taking time to do what makes you happy. Even if it's only 10 minutes a day, turning off your phone, exercising, meditating or listening to music can prepare you when stressful events occur.
- When you find yourself in a conversation where you may be getting angry, walk away and take some time away from the situation. This will allow you to cool down, and provide you with the time you need to reflect on the issue. You may want to ask yourself in those stressful situations how important they are in the long run.
- If you are feeling overwhelmed with your schedule or workload, reevaluate it and make sure you're not doing too much. You should feel challenged or busy without being overwhelmed in life.
- Practice gratitude by identifying three things every day you are grateful for.
- Use self-talk to help you see things from a more positive perspective.
- Learn to forgive others and let go of any negative feelings and resentment.

- Improve your communication skills, which will help you to reduce stress when embroiled in a conflict.

Knowing that our past informs our present, and our present shapes our future, we can work at staying present in the moment. Working on the pain from your past is important so that you may learn to reclaim your power in the present, and make healthy choices for the future. Some people may not be able to go this route alone, and having the support of a good therapist or coach who is caring and compassionate will promote healing and empowerment.

Should I Go or Should I Stay

Deciding to stay or to go in a toxic relationship can be difficult, and there will be many obstacles no matter what the decision is. It can be difficult to leave someone whom you still love. Even within a toxic relationship, you may still feel love for this person. Once you make the decision to leave and are on your own, you will have time to reflect on your life and situation. From this perspective, you will begin to develop a more independent self and become empowered with the knowledge that you were able to achieve independence.

Occasionally when one person is ready to move on and out of a relationship, the other person will use blame and guilt to try and force the other to stay. They may even threaten suicide to manipulate the person into staying. Know and understand that these tactics are used to make you feel sorry for them and stay.

Finances are a big deterrent for women in regard to going or staying, especially if the husband is the breadwinner in the relationship. He may threaten to cut you and the children off from any money if you decide to end the relationship. Many women who have no skills or job possibilities, or no family or friends to help support them, may feel helpless and stuck in their relationship. With nowhere to go and without the possibility of work, many women feel there is no other option but to stay in the relationship.

Depending on cultural and spiritual beliefs, many women are afraid to break up their family. They would rather accept the abuse and make the sacrifice by staying in order to raise the children with two parents. The father may also threaten the mother that he will turn the children against her for breaking up the family. Many women are afraid of having joint custody with the father, and fear retaliation when leaving the children alone with him.

There can be issues with shame and guilt about being in a toxic relationship. Women who are in a toxic relationship usually don't tell anyone, and leaving would force them to disclose their deepest, darkest secrets. If your significant other is a high-ranking professional or political figure in the community, you may not want to jeopardize his status by revealing the toxic relationship.

People in toxic relationships often feel guilty and blame themselves for the abusive behavior of their partners. You may hear that if it weren't for your incompetence and lame behavior, they wouldn't be in this predicament. They may suggest that you "try harder" to be better, but nothing is ever good enough and the toxic behavior will continue.

Many times women feel powerless and too overwhelmed to consider leaving the relationship. They may feel isolated from their friends and family, and don't want to ask for help. Feelings of sadness, guilt and shame can also add to feelings of depression, which lead to a lack of confidence and self-esteem. All of these feelings add to the feeling of being stuck in the relationship.

Intention Setting

As you work through your coping strategies and practice mindfulness, set an intention to heal at the beginning of each session. By setting an intention, you are making the deliberate decision to create something new or to change something in your life. Setting an intention sets in motion the stage for change to begin. Begin to think about how and what you want to change in your relationship and life.

Setting an intention is the starting point for you to begin to gain clarity on what is important to you. Everything in life begins with an intention. Whether it's what's for dinner tonight, or what movie to see, it all starts with an intention. Your power comes from the focused awareness on the intention you set. Wayne Dyer said, "Intentions create reality."

As you practice your mindfulness, reflect back onto your intention, and begin to think about small actions to work toward your goal. When your thoughts are flowing in the same direction as your intention, you give power and energy to the intention and can create it faster and easier. Whatever your decision is, to change will require both being and doing.

Being Versus Doing

Being is your intention, and the values and qualities you would like to emanate. Doing is developing your plan of action through daily small steps. Small steps lead to big changes. For example, if your decision is to leave like Brenda, you will want to work daily toward achieving that goal by planning financially and logistically, and getting support of family and friends. Or perhaps you would like to stay with your husband. By doing small things daily for each other, you can improve your relationship and help enhance your interpersonal dynamics. Things like checking in with each other during the day, or providing loving companionship and support to each other in the evenings, will help to facilitate a better relationship. Directing your energy and actions toward the intention you aspire to will provide the foundation for you to balance your life and achieve your dream.

Connecting to Conscious Choice

When you connect to conscious choice, you will be able to distance yourself from the toxic relationship, and observe it as a witness. Being a witness allows you to observe the situation without feeling like a victim. Visualize standing above yourself and watching your life go by as in a movie. What changes would you like to make? How could you empower the woman on the screen? From this perspective, you can also separate from the toxic behavior and view it from a different viewpoint, perhaps beginning to understand why it's happening and offering compassion for his issues.

Sophie's Experience

Sophie began to travel with her daughter, first to London and then, Paris. Following their European trips, they started going to California for summers, and that experience revolutionized her worldview. Suddenly Sophie was seeing life through a different lens; one that allowed her to enjoy experiences and sensations that were not familiar to her as a wife and homemaker.

Every time Sophie returned to her home to her husband, she was miserable. Sophie knew the veil had been lifted, and once she had walked out through that door she could not turn back. Her husband was relentless in his pursuit to keep the family together and used every conceivable tactic to get her back. Once Sophie left for good, she made the decision not to speak with her husband anymore. Without speaking to him, he no longer had the opportunity of manipulating her with his suicidal threats, or making her feel guilty for breaking up the family and abandoning him. It was only then that she could begin to live her best life, not being influenced by him any longer.

Sophie was finally feeling she could live an authentic life on her own terms, without the criticism and opinions of others. When she finally understood that the universe works with her, and not against her, she was able to trust in herself and her decision.

Making the decision to change is one of the most difficult challenges anyone can face. Understanding the complex patterns of human behavior, and using the GRACE methodology outlined, will make your journey easier.

Spirit Work

Think about what buried dreams you might be keeping within. Imagining you had no fear and you had endless amounts of courage and strength, what are your deepest dreams? Journal them and include ones that you might be able to accomplish. Keep in mind that you can do anything you set your mind to, so remember there are no limits here. Feel free to share them with others. Here are some examples:

- Write an article for your local newspaper or magazine
- Study French Cooking
- Learn to speak Italian
- Visit Greece and the ancient ruins
- Tour the pyramids of Egypt
- Go on a safari in Africa
- Join an acting group
- Join a band
- Run a marathon
- Take a yoga class
- Volunteer for a local organization that could use your talents
- Write a mystery novel
- Meditate for 5 minutes everyday

Chapter 7

EMPOWERMENT THROUGH EMBRACING CHANGE THROUGH MOVEMENT

The empowered woman is powerful beyond measure and beautiful beyond description.
— **Steve Maraboli**

Mindful Movement

I consider the body as a microcosm of life. For example, if you are stiff and inflexible, you may embody these same qualities in your life: being unwilling to change and compromise in many situations. Learning and practicing mindfulness and mindful movement will begin to provide balance in your life, while increasing strength, courage, and self-awareness. The flexibility you gain in the body will be the flexibility you can apply to your life. Your life will become easier, as your mind becomes more adaptable and resilient. Every challenge you face will become a growth opportunity.

Learn to listen to your body's intuitive awareness, which will connect you to your feminine knowledge and truth. Staying in present-moment awareness and connecting with your body will allow you to begin to understand who you are, and that you are not just your thoughts.

Mindful movement allows one to stay present in the here and now to evaluate what is occurring in the present moment. Our bodies have a consciousness and a connection to our mind. Our muscles tend to hold our emotions, and by becoming flexible through mindful movement, we are able to release the muscles and emotions held there. As our bodies become more flexible, it helps our minds to become more flexible, and that opens us to change. It is through this openness that you can begin to contemplate and embrace change and make your decision on whether to stay or go.

My client Gina was always into physical fitness, but it wasn't until she began practicing mindful movement that her life transformed. Changes are subtle and progress slowly at first, so her transformation wasn't evident immediately, but she knew something was feeling different. Practicing mindful movement helped Gina to connect with her inner self, and begin to understand obstacles and past behaviors that were hindering her life. Through her mindful movement practice, she was able to gain confidence and strength, increase her self-esteem and find her true authentic self. This was so empowering for her that she was able to begin to set boundaries in her relationship. This one small action was big enough to save her relationship.

Most people begin a mindful movement practice with having a beautiful body as their goal, and a healthy body is certainly important in life. For our intensive purposes, we will be practicing mindfulness and mindful movement to provide a spiritual road map, to help you embrace and live your destiny. Beyond the spiritual benefits discussed, mindful movement will aid you in discovering how to love and accept your body, while also improving posture and muscle tone.

Your body awareness will increase through mindful movement practice, which will increase your self-awareness. An increase in self-awareness makes it is easier to follow your spiritual road map to meet your intentions and goals. When your awareness is outside of your experience, it's difficult to see and change circumstances. Expanding your awareness through mindful movement will allow you to bring your experience into your consciousness and create the change you need.

Recent studies now indicate we can change the brain through a process called neuroplasticity. Mindfulness and mindful movement will create new pathways in the brain. These new pathways will lay the groundwork for new habits, which ultimately lead to changes in behavior.

Mindful movement is a practice of meditation in motion, and is an exercise performed with awareness to help you live smarter and to create space for choice. This type of movement provides introspection to connect you to your authentic self where spiritual energy and power reside. This is not power over people, but power over you. As you establish your power, and move toward your deeper spiritual center, you will develop balance and connection to the values and intentions you set in your life.

Sages of India created mindful movement postures known as asana (poses) over 5,000 years ago. They were modeled after nature and illustrate the principal of evolution. Some asana are named after animals, fish, and trees, and bring us into attunement with nature. The goal of mindful movement practice is happiness, through balancing life-energies. When your life is in balance, you can be happy and flourish.

Most of us live in our heads, and we need to come down into our bodies to connect the mind, body and spirit. People who are stuck in their heads have difficulty in feeling bodily sensations. This creates a disconnection between the mind, body and spirit. Mindful movement is one of the best ways to begin to connect the mind, body and spirit, through connection and attention to our body and breath.

Our bodies are never concerned with the past or future, and this allows connection to our consciousness to always be in the present moment. Connecting with consciousness allows us to know what emotions the body is feeling. This in turn leads us to awakening our true spirit and becoming the best versions of ourselves.

Attention to your intuition allows you to live through spirit by virtue of the body. Carl Jung—a famous psychologist—describes intuition as "unconscious perception that taps into implicit processes and knowledge in the body and brain." By practicing mindfulness and mindful movement, intuition is strengthened by the ability to focus on physical sensations and thoughts.

Living from a space of intuition can be inspiring, and provides access to your internal compass in life. Intuition allows you to connect and utilize the deep wisdom of your body, and live life with integrity, in mind, body and spirit. Here is where you can thrive following your life course, gain energy, and connect to source. You may notice an increase in creativity, joy, compassion and kindness toward yourself and others as you practice. It feels good and peaceful to live from this space.

Through the practice of mindful movement, the body is stretched and relaxed, tension is relieved and freshly oxygenated blood revitalizes the organs of the body, including the brain. Relieving tension in the body relaxes and calms the mind, while releasing tension in the organs induces stillness. Reaching stillness of the mind allows one to perceive the superconscious, and thus find the harmonious balance of their entire being.

The following mindful movement practice is designed to help you to gain clarity on whether to stay or go in your relationship. This is accomplished through introspection gained during the practice and connecting with the intelligence of the body. As you focus on your body, you begin to notice feelings prior to the movement, and subtle shifts in your emotions, impulses and intention. This creates the space for choice and the opportunity for change. With practice you will take this wisdom off the mat, and learn how to apply it in your life.

Our focus will be using 10 particular poses that will train and strengthen the mind body connection. The needs of the spirit are met through meeting the needs of the body through mindful movement.

The names of the pose will be listed first, with the meaning and benefits of each following. Practice can be done any time of day, and should be practiced daily if possible.

Mindful Movement Practice

Easy Pose

Mindful meditation is practiced sitting in easy pose.

- In a seated position bend the legs and cross the right shin over the left shin
- Draw the knees closer together

- Place the hands beside the hips, press the fingertips into the floor to lift the trunk vertically
- Rest the hands on the knees
- Breathe for 5 breaths (or longer)

Mountain Pose

When in mountain pose you are standing strong, and mountain-like. Feeling the strength and solidity of the body are the two qualities you can take off the mat and into your life.

- Standing erect with feet together, the heels and big toes should be touching

- Tighten the knees lifting up the kneecaps, stretching up the muscles at the back of the thighs
- Stomach is in, chest is forward and spine is stretched straight up
- Distribute the weight of the body evenly on both feet
- Place your arms next to the body with palms turned outward
- Follow the breath as you relax the mind standing in mountain pose

Tree Pose

Tree pose will increase confidence and create a more positive level of self-esteem. While also opening the heart, it will increase your sense of well-being.

- Stand in mountain pose
- Bend the right leg at the knee and place the foot at the root of the left thigh
- Rest the foot on the left thigh, with toes pointing down
- If you have difficulty balancing, you can place the foot on the shin and floor
- Balance on the left leg. Join the palms and raise the arms straight overhead
- Stay for 5 breaths breathing deeply. Lower the arms and separate the palms, straighten the right leg and come back into standing in mountain pose
- Repeat the pose standing on the right leg, placing the left heel at the root of the right thigh. Stay for same amount of time (5 breaths)
- Return to mountain pose and rest

Warrior 1 Pose

Warrior 1 is a pose that helps to develop concentration, groundedness, balance and strength.

- Begin standing in mountain pose
- Raise both arms above the head and stretch up, joining the palms
- Take a deep inhalation and spread the legs apart sideways 4-4 1/2 feet
- Turn to the right and place the right foot at 90 degrees to the right and the left foot in slightly to the right
- Bend the right knee bringing the right thigh parallel to the floor
- The bent knee should not extend beyond the ankle, but should be in line with the heel
- Left leg is stretched out straight
- The face, chest and right knee should face the same way as the right foot.
- Gently gaze up at the palms stretched above the head
- Hold for 5 breaths
- Repeat on the left side reversing all processes
- Come back into mountain pose

Warrior 2 Pose

Warrior 2 pose develops concentration, groundedness, balance, stability and strength—all qualities we need in life to be strong, stable and gain clarity on our needs

- Begin standing in mountain pose
- Jump the feet 4-4 1/2 feet apart with arms stretched out to the side
- Turn the right foot out 90 degrees and the left foot in 15 degrees
- Extend the trunk upward
- Exhale and bend the right leg to a right angle
- Firm your left leg by pressing the left heel into the floor
- Tuck your tailbone slightly, and keep your weight balanced on both feet
- The upper body is centered over the hips, keeping the torso evenly long
- Turn your head to the right and look out over your fingers
- Stay for 5 breaths Inhale and come up and repeat steps on the left side, reversing all processes

Triangle Pose

Benefits include mental and physical equilibrium and reducing stress and anxiety. Having a calm mind and body can help in times of stress.

- Stand straight and separate your feet about 3 1/2 to 4 feet apart
- Turn your right foot out 90 degrees and the left foot in by 15 degrees
- Press your feet into the ground while keeping your body balanced equally on both feet
- Inhale deeply and as you exhale bend your body to the right, downward from the hips, keep the waist straight, and allow your left hand to come up in the air while bringing your right hand down to the floor.
- Keep both arms in a straight line

- Rest your right hand on your shin, ankle or floor outside the right foot
- Stretch your left arm toward the ceiling, in line with the tops of your shoulders
- Keep your head in a neutral position or turn it to the left allowing the eyes to gaze softly at the left palm
- Stretch and be steady, breathing deeply, while relaxing the body
- On the inhalation come up, bringing your arms down to your side and straighten your feet
- Repeat steps on the left side, reversing all processes

Half Moon Pose

Benefits of Half Moon Pose include strengthening thighs, ankles, spine, and buttocks, while improving balance and strength.

- Perform Triangle pose on the right side with the left hand resting on the hip

- Exhale and bend the right knee and bring the left foot forward slightly in toward the right foot
- Place the fingertips of the right hand on the floor 1 foot front of the right leg and in line with the leg
- Simultaneously raise the left leg, keeping it extended and straightening the right knee and stretching the right leg up
- Straighten the right arm and stretch the left arm up and in line with the right arm
- Lift up the left hip and take it back so that it rests over the right hip
- Turn the head and look up
- Stay for 5 breaths
- Inhale and come up. Repeat on the left side

Downward-Facing Dog

Benefits of Downward-Facing Dog include incredible balance for the body and mind.

- On all fours, take the knees 1 foot apart
- Tuck the toes under, and on the inhale raise the hips
- Keep the palms on the mat and arms straight
- Keep the legs straight and make the knees firm
- Without losing the height of the hips, stretch the heels down
- Moving thighs and shins back to bring the weight onto the backs of the legs and heels
- Relax the head and neck
- Stay for 5 breaths

Forward Bend

Benefits include relief of stress, anxiety, anger and irritability. It acts to calm and still the mind.

- Sit in a seated position with the legs together and stretched out in front of you
- On an exhalation lean forward, extending the arms, and hold the feet

- Inhale and pull on the feet and extend the trunk up from the pubis
- Stretch both sides of the trunk and open the chest
- Exhale and bend the elbows outward, and lean down taking the trunk toward the legs
- Extend the front body toward the feet
- Rest the head on the thighs or shin
- Breath evenly staying for 5 breaths

Corpse Pose
Benefits of Corpse Pose include stress relief, calming the brain and relief of mild depression

- Sit in a seated position with the legs together and stretched out in front of you
- Lean back onto the elbows
- Lie down lowering the back vertebra by vertebra
- Place a pillow or blanket under the head
- Settle the back onto the floor.
- Extend the arms next to the body at a 45 degree angle to the body
- Relax the torso, arms and legs
- Close the eyes and keep the breath normal

- Try not to let the mind wander and keep the attention on the body
- Keep the body still and relax
- Allow the body to sink into the ground
- Stay quietly for 5-10 minutes
- Slowly open the eyes, bend the legs, turn to the right side and stay for a moment
- Gently bring yourself up to a seated position

Practicing mindful movement at its most basic level is about change and empowerment. Opening yourself up to knowing you have the strength, courage and power to choose whatever is going to make you happiest in life. The clarity you are able to gain through mindful movement will help you to have a perspective you may not have had previously. When we learn awareness through bodily sensations, emotions and thoughts, we can observe, reflect and act on making positive changes to empower ourselves.

Spirit Work

This week's spirit work is to practice mindful movement. Try to practice on a daily basis, starting slowly and working your way up to 30 minutes. As you practice, notice any bodily sensations and where you may be feeling them. Pay attention to any thoughts you may be thinking, and be gentle and compassionate toward yourself. Just do what you can. Starting your mindful movement with 5 minutes of mindfulness is a great way of getting centered and grounded before beginning.

Keeping a journal as you practice can help you to keep track of your progress.

Chapter 8

CHANGING THE
STORY OF YOUR LIFE

Imagine a new story for your life and start living it.
–Paul Coelho

C hanging the story of your life requires you to take your happiness and well-being into your own hands. No matter what your past experience has been, you can change it by making empowered choices. Now that you have decided that toxic behavior will not be tolerated in your life, you are ready to take action.

By rebuilding your self-esteem and confidence through the skills you've learned, you can make choices that begin to bring joy and happiness back into your life. Taking control allows you take personal responsibility for your life, and to make your own choices and decisions living according to your own values. This can be both empowering and scary at the same time.

You may be asking yourself, "Where do I begin?" Throughout this book, you have been examining your life, and by now you should have a good idea of whether to stay or go. It can be frightening to make such a big decision, but as you take back control, your fears will begin to fade. Your life will be more enjoyable and effortless when you create it on your own terms.

Staying in the Relationship

Deciding to stay may sound easier, but it can be just as difficult as leaving. It requires the mindfulness to understand what you need and want in your relationship, and the ability to communicate that to your significant other. If you have been living a life of fear, control and domination, it will take great strength and courage to move into a position of control for yourself. I have seen many women work through these issues, and begin to have better relationships. For the women who have stayed and changed the relationship dynamic, almost all of them tell me they would never be able to go back to living in a toxic relationship again. These women were able to communicate boundaries, and explain what their needs were effectively. As they changed, their partners changed and the relationship improved for both of them.

You will never be able to be happy without changing the current dynamics in your relationship. You may be experiencing pain from the past, and in order to move forward, you must be willing to forgive. Clinging to past hurt and anger will not help you or the relationship. You may feel the need to talk about past transgressions, and let your partner know that you forgive them for all the pain they have caused you.

Staying in the relationship requires you to share with your partner that you are not going to settle for anything less than an equal, respectful and healthy relationship. Your partner must know that you have changed, and it's important for you to share what your boundaries are, and the consequences when he crosses them. You are the only one who can improve your circumstances, and change the way you act in the relationship. Using the techniques and practices in this book, you can assert your needs and improve your relationship.

Remember a relationship is a living phenomenon, and must be nurtured and cared for. It will take effort and time to reconnect with your partner, and it takes both partners working toward a respectful, healthy and intimate relationship.

Here are a few tips to make your relationship the best it can be:

- Both partners should be committed to making their relationship their #1 priority
- You communicate openly and honestly with each other
- Use your self-awareness to foster emotional intimacy with each other
- Spend quality time together and be able to laugh together
- Become more affectionate with each other
- Be there for each other in a loving, supportive way

- Love yourself—true love requires you love yourself first before extending it to others
- Accept each other and your differences
- Address conflicts quickly
- Stay open and honest with each other

This will take practice, and in the beginning may be an everyday struggle to push past the fear and doubt of being able to reclaim your power. With every small step you make, you empower yourself and you will begin to see how these small changes start to change the bigger overall picture. The only way to get to the other side is going through the changes and work required to have a happy and loving relationship.

My client Judy's husband Alex was controlling, angry and bitter toward her, and she never understood why. When Alex was diagnosed with kidney cancer, he became exponentially worse toward her. He was always condescending and angry, but now it was completely unbearable for her. Judy could endure the toxic behavior no more, and told him he was either going to change or it was over. This was the lowest point in Alex's life, and he needed Judy. Alex heard the wake-up call and decided to change. It was a long, hard road for the two of them, but Judy was able to communicate what she wanted and needed to feel loved and appreciated. She was also able to set boundaries. Because of Alex's condition, he made the changes necessary to save their relationship. Today Judy and Alex just returned from a romantic European holiday. Their relationship is not perfect, but both Judy and Alex are glad they stayed together and made the changes necessary to save their relationship.

Leaving the Relationship

If you have been doing the work, and know you are ready to leave, it takes courage and strength to follow this path. Not having a sense of what the future will bring can be frightening, and you may still be under the spell of no matter how bad the situation, it could be worse without them.

In order to leave your toxic relationship, there are some elements to the relationship that you must believe to be able to finally walk away. Know and understand that they may never be able to change in the way you need or want. No matter what you say or do, they won't change. You are not their #1 priority, and they are incapable of having a healthy relationship. They may change on a short-term basis, but they still won't be the person you think they are. When they know you want to leave, they can be malicious and manipulative, and they will do everything and anything to keep you in the relationship. I have had many clients tell me their partners have even threatened suicide. Fortunately, they were just idle threats and manipulative tactics. You deserve to be happy, and you will be. It's important to know that something bigger and better is waiting for you on the other side.

Many clients ask me how they should tell them, and what should they say. It's important for them to understand this is not a discussion. You are telling them how you feel, and what you are going to do. If they sense any uncertainty or doubt, they will jump on it immediately. They will then try to convince you to stay by preying on your fears and insecurities. Some women feel better having a support system with a family member or friend with them when they tell them they are leaving. Remember this is not a discussion, and you don't have to clarify your decision at this moment. You may get closure at a later time, to avoid an argument.

Prior to communicating that you are leaving, it's important to have your belongings prepared, packed and moved to avoid having to see them again. Seeing them again opens the conversation for you to stay, and perhaps to offer forgiveness. They may have manipulated and talked their way back into your life in the past, but now is different. You have a plan, and the strength and courage to take your life back.

In the beginning it will be a difficult path, and you may feel lonely. You will miss your partner and the security you felt, but know you are not missing him—you are just missing having a partner. You may be tempted to go back, or just even call or text to see how they are doing. This is a very big mistake, and when these feelings arise, you may need external support. Have a support system set up through friends and family who you trust and who care about you.

You may feel embarrassed and ashamed about your past situation and the pain and hurt you endured. Remember none of your friends or family will feel that way; they want to be there to support and love you as you return from the self-imposed prison you were held in for so long. It's time to break free from the self-limiting blockades and move forward into a successful new life.

The Road to Recovery

Coming back from a toxic relationship can be difficult. Emotional and mental wounds are hard to recover from, and you will need to address them. If not, these feelings will grow and fester and manifest in other ways in the future.

Aftereffects of abusive relationships include:

- You may be suspicious of any member of the opposite gender
- You may begin to hate them and not trust anyone
- You may distrust your own choices
- You may have flashbacks to a past traumatic event
- You may feel negatively toward everyday events or anything that reminds you of your partner
- You may become obsessed with the relationship, and blame yourself
- You may feel anxiety and be irritable

If you are experiencing any of these aftereffects, you may want to consult with a psychotherapist or relationship coach. This will help you get back into your life and reconnect with the people and things that made you happy.

From my own personal experience I was afraid to tell my partner it was over. It wasn't always bad, but it was a slow, insidious process. Similar to a frog placed in a pot of cold water, eventually you end up as soup.

Over the years, my sense of self had completely disappeared; I was financially dependent and scared to leave. His anger and outbursts scared me into compliance, but I was at a point where I knew I had to do something to keep my sanity. I knew that I could not ignore the inner voice in my head, and continue to live a life that was not authentic for me.

I let my inner voice take over, and sat down and told him it was over. I was truly frightened of the uncertainty ahead. He was never physically abusive, but was emotionally and mentally controlling. When I finally told him he seemed to be shocked, and couldn't believe it was over. I experienced the same emotions many of you might be feeling; frightened and worried where I was going to go and how I was going to live. When we are ready to move on, somehow we find the strength and courage. It's a process—one that is very personal and only you can know when you are ready.

If your relationship feels like you are being held in a psychological prison, know you can take back your life. By changing your mindset through development of self-awareness, you can break free of the metaphorical bars keeping you imprisoned. Through knowing your values, setting your goals and practicing mindfulness and mindful movement, you are empowering yourself for change. We all have the capability to take charge of our lives with GRACE, strength and confidence. It's your turn now.

CONCLUSION

*No matter who you are, no matter what you did,
no matter where you've come from, you can always
change, become a better version of yourself.*
– Madonna

After working with my client Rachel through the GRACE system, she chose to move out of her marriage, and into her own life. She felt too much contempt and hate to continue on in her relationship, or to try to stick it out and repair the damage. Rachel had endured over 20 years of being in a toxic relationship, and it took her longer than 5 years to complete her divorce. During that time, she needed much strength and courage to complete the GRACE process. She relied on her mindfulness and mindful movement

111

practice for strength, courage and resiliency. She even confided in me that she thought her introspective practices helped her more than psychotherapy.

Once Rachel learned and understood the complex dynamics behind her relationship, she made the decision to work toward changing her situation. That included learning to transform her self-loathing into self-love, self-compassion and self-respect. She began to make choices every day to begin healing from the excruciatingly painful hatred and denigration she suffered.

It was only through building her confidence and self-esteem that Rachel could move forward in a positive direction. Through Rachel's practice of her soul work, she was able to learn to love herself, forgive past transgressions of others, and live an authentic life. Rachel made small choices every day that led to big changes in her life. This was only possible through learning and developing self-love, since our choices are inseparably linked to our own self-worth. She was able to face her fears, break through her feelings of denial and make peace with her pain to come fully into the greatest expression of herself.

Working toward self-actualization, Rachel was finally able to connect with her authentic self and discover her true potential. It was from this vantage point that she knew she didn't have to accept her toxic relationship or the way her life existed. As the icy feelings of detachment, depression and anxiety began to melt, Rachel was able to make decisions that felt right for her. She instinctually began to understand what her needs and wants were. It was at this point she vowed never to feel controlled, shamed or unhappy in her life again. Today

Rachel is living the life she's always dreamed of in Florida, and she has even earned an advanced degree.

Should you decide to stay, just know that love never hurts or holds anyone back from growing. If you feel you need to grow, it might mean walking away from the toxic person or environment. You can always leave the door open, and let them know if they are willing to meet you on your terms you may be there for them. Use GRACE and love to set boundaries, and let them decide where they want to stand in your world. If they decide they can't treat you the way you deserve, the relationship ended not because of your lack of love, but their choice. You deserve to be treated with love, respect and honor.

My wish for you is that you find inspiration in the stories and exercises in this book. Take the information and apply it in your life and work on what makes you truly happy. Happiness can be a reality for you right now; you just have to decide to take action for yourself.

Whether you decide to stay in your relationship, or move on like Rachel, know that you have the power. Remember, *"You've always had the power my dear, you just had to learn it for yourself."* Glenda the Good Witch, In The Wizard of Oz

Know that you have what it takes to turn your life into the life of your dreams. Realize in your heart you deserve nothing less than being happy in this life, and you are the only one who can make that choice. You are full of potential for the future, and emotional freedom and happiness are waiting on the other side.

ACKNOWLEDGMENTS

I gratefully acknowledge my book coach Angela for sharing her infinite knowledge and wisdom, and motivating me to write forward in the face of adversity. My friends and family whose love and support were there for me throughout the project, and my bestie who gave me valuable insight in Too Good To Go, Too Bad To Stay (you know who you are). Finally, to Roxy who provided unconditional love and support, and has been a source of light, love and happiness in my life since I adopted her.

To the Morgan James Publishing team: Special thanks to David Hancock, CEO & Founder for believing in me and my message. To my Author Relations Manager, Margo Toulouse thanks for making the process seamless and easy. Many more thanks to everyone else, but especially Jim Howard, Bethany Marshall, and Nickcole Watkins.

ABOUT THE AUTHOR

Joanne is a psychotherapist, author, certified yoga instructor and spiritual healer. She has dedicated her life to helping others achieve spiritual and emotional well-being through introspection and mindfulness. Joanne has a Bachelor of Arts degree in Psychology, and a Master of Arts degree in Counseling Psychology. Her work focuses on emotional healing, which supports the mind, body, and spirit connection. Joanne also works as a private consultant, helping to empower people to reconnect with their authentic selves, and make positive changes in their lives. When not sharing tea with close friends, or walking her dog Roxy, Joanne can be found on the beach enjoying the sun and surf. Join the Movement at www. JoanneKingCoaching.com or email **Joanne@ JoanneKingCoaching.com**

THANK YOU

Thank you for reading *Too Good To Go, Too Bad To Stay.* You're ready to begin your journey to creating a better life for yourself. It's time to create clarity, joy, and happiness, through the GRACE process.

As a special thank you, please visit my website www. *JoanneKingCoaching.com* for a free download of Appendix A and all the meditations at the end of each chapter. You may also sign up for a complimentary clarity session to help you begin your journey. Details can be found at **www.JoanneKingCoaching.com**

Morgan James makes all of our titles available
through the Library for All Charity Organization.

www.LibraryForAll.org

9 781683 508151